"A man wishes to conquer at the Olympic games... You must do everything according to rule, eat according to strict orders, abstain from delicacies, exercise yourself as you are bid at appointed times, in heat, in cold, you must not drink cold water, nor wine as you choose; in a word, you must deliver yourself up to the exercise master as you do to the physician, and then proceed to the contest. And sometimes you will strain the hand, put the ankle out of joint, swallow much dust, sometimes be flogged, and after all this be defeated."

Epictetus, Enchiridion, c.50 – c.135 AD

Human Race Object Guide
Editors: Kitty Chilcott and Malcolm MacCallum

Designed by CMYK Design

Printed by J Thomson Colour Printers

www.scotlandandmedicine.com
humanrace.org.uk

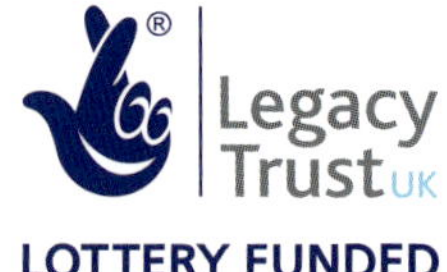

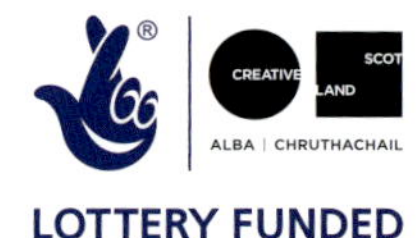

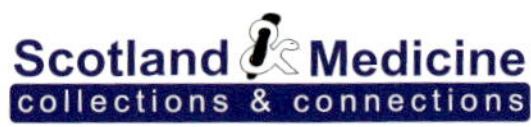

Human Race Tour, Scotland 2012

STIRLING
2 MARCH – 13 APRIL 2012
Pathfoot Gallery, University of Stirling
and The Peak at Stirling Sports Village

ABERDEEN
20 APRIL – 18 MAY
MacRobert Building, University of Aberdeen
and Aberdeen Sports Village

INVERNESS
25 MAY – 7 JULY
Inverness Museum and Art Gallery

EDINBURGH
21 JULY – 9 SEPTEMBER
City Art Centre
and Royal Commonwealth Pool

DUNDEE
21 SEPTEMBER – 10 NOVEMBER
Lamb Gallery, University of Dundee
and Institute of Sport and Exercise, University of Dundee

Lead Curator: Malcolm MacCallum
Director of Heritage RCSEd: Chris Henry
Art Curator: Prof Andrew Patrizio
Researcher: Dr Joanne O'Hara
Project Manager (Marketing & Development): Kitty Chilcott
Exhibition Design and Production: NORD - Northern Office for Research & Design

FOREWORD

This book, along with the **Human Race** exhibition, is the result of funding from Legacy Trust UK and Creative Scotland National Lottery Fund, and is a Scotland & Medicine: Collections & Connections Partnership initiative. The exhibition uses Scottish collections and newly commissioned artworks to explore and explain the history, culture and science of sport and exercise medicine, and its impact on the human body.

The Scotland & Medicine Partnership was established in 2004 to improve access to and promote the knowledge of health and medical related collections and to increase public awareness of Scotland's global impact on the history and development of medicine. Twenty-three organisations make up the Partnership and include many of Scotland's leading museums, galleries, archives and university special collections. The Royal College of Surgeons of Edinburgh (RCSEd) is the lead partner.

Since 2004 the Partnership has encouraged people of all ages to be informed, inspired and involved in Scotland's medical heritage through exciting multi-diciplinary projects. The **Human Race** exhibition will continue to build excitement and interest bringing together medical collections, researchers, practitioners and creative artists that will give people the opportunity of exploring the culture of sport from a unique perspective.

Human Race has been funded by Legacy Trust UK, creating a lasting impact from the London 2012 Olympic and Paralympic Games by funding ideas and local talent to inspire creativity across the UK. It is also forms part of Creative Scotland's London 2012 and Glasgow 2014 Cultural Programme and the Year of Creative Scotland.

INTRODUCTION

The Human Race touring exhibition uses objects from Scottish collections dating from the Bronze Age to the latest body imaging techniques and sports equipment to explore and explain centuries of developments in sport and exercise medicine.

The objects have been selected from museums, libraries, universities and archives as well as private collections and sports manufacturers. Many have never been on public display before. The most complete version of the exhibition will be on show at the City Art Centre in Edinburgh. A smaller version of the exhibition will be on display at other venues.

Entries in this guide are organised by exhibition theme. Objects which are not displayed at some exhibition venues may be viewed by contacting the local institution or collection holder. Further information about Scottish medical collections can be found at the back of this guide.

LOOKING AND UNDERSTANDING

From early engravings, sculptures and paintings, to photographs, film and digital imaging, depictions of the body in sport have changed over time. During the 19th century, the development of photography allowed the active body to be represented more accurately, and a single frame of human movement could be captured. With the introduction of film in the early 20th century, a detailed analysis of the athlete in motion could be undertaken for the first time. Pioneers in motion analysis studies, such as Thomas McClurg Anderson (1899–1980) from Motherwell, began to use film as a tool to examine and improve athletic technique, but also as a way to help prevent injuries caused by playing sport.

Advances in medical imaging have allowed scientists and the medical profession to develop a greater understanding of the human body. Today, every part of the athlete, from bones and tendons, to an individual muscle fibre, can be analysed. X-rays and magnetic resonance imaging (MRI), both of which were pioneered in Scotland, have improved the diagnosis of injury and helped to ensure that athletes receive better and more informed treatment, allowing a quicker return to competitive sport.

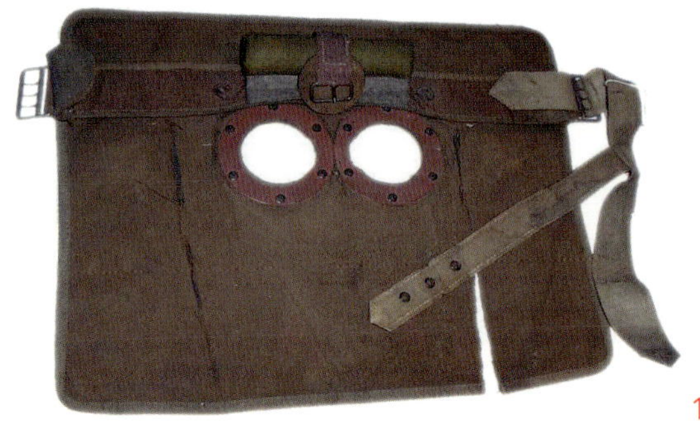

1

MRI scan of an ankle

Magnetic resonance imaging (MRI) is a non-invasive procedure that uses powerful magnets and radio waves to construct pictures of the body by targeting the body's own atoms. Professor John Mallard (born 1927) is one of the inventors of MRI. At Aberdeen he was responsible for some of the major developments which led to the first clinically useful MRI scans of patients.

Courtesy of the University of Aberdeen

Glass and lead-lined protective goggles [1]

Dr George Pirie (1863–1929) began his investigations on X-rays at Dundee Royal Infirmary in 1896. He continued his work there until 1925, when he was forced to retire due to ill health brought about by his long exposure to X-rays. These goggles were used by Pirie as protection from radiation damage. Unfortunately they were too late to prevent him from losing one eye and most of the sight in his other one.

University of Dundee Museum Services, Tayside Medical History Museum, DUNUC4326

Bottle of mustard oil

In 1905, after ten years of exposure to X-rays, Dr Pirie began to experience what he called "trouble" in his hands; he rubbed mustard oil onto his skin to help ease the pain. Radiation exposure eventually led to his hands being amputated.

University of Dundee Museum Services, Tayside Medical History Museum, DUNUC4289

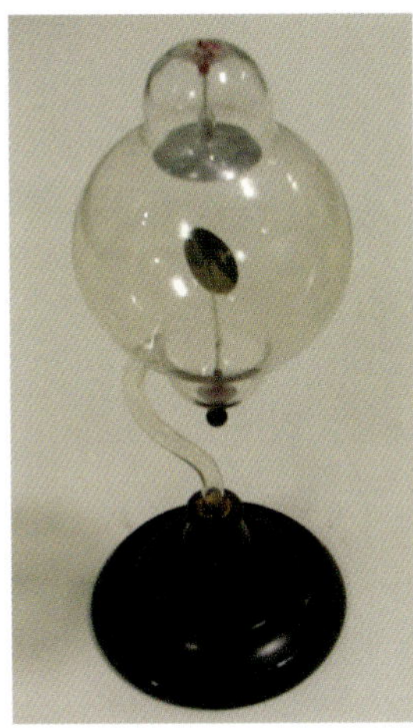

2

Experimental X-ray tube, c.1890s [2]

X-rays are generated when a stream of electrons from the cathode of an evacuated electrical discharge tube strikes a target inside the tube. This early X-ray tube was used at Dundee Royal Infirmary during the late 1890s. X-rays continue to be used to diagnose orthopaedic sporting injuries but, due to dangers of overexposure from radiation, are now not used as widely for the diagnosis of soft-tissue injuries.

University of Dundee Museum Services, Tayside Medical History Museum, DUNUC4329

Siemens Sonostat 631 Therapeutic Ultrasound Generator with transducer, 1957

Ultrasound for medical use was pioneered by Professor Ian Donald at the University of Glasgow. It is best known as a diagnostic tool for use in obstetric visualisation, showing the human foetus inside the womb. Over the last 50 years, many sports club physiotherapists and doctors believed that ultrasound also had a therapeutic use for the treatment of sports injuries. Ultrasound machines (which use high-energy sound waves) were often used to stimulate blood flow to the affected part of the athlete's body or to help improve flexibility in damaged joints. Ultrasound also seems to help the healing process of fractured bones, but there is little evidence that it speeds up the healing process in other types of sports injury.

Courtesy of the British Medical Ultrasound Society Historical Collection

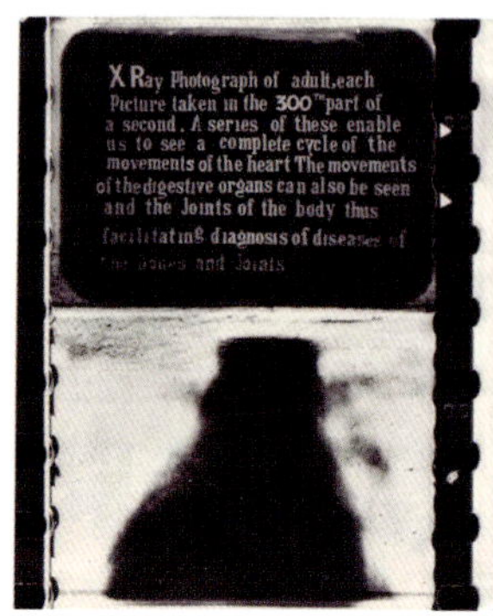

3

Images of the knee joint

Advances in medical imaging have allowed doctors to diagnose sports injuries with increasing accuracy. These scans show the four main ligaments of the knee, including the anterior cruciate ligament (ACL). The ACL is the most vulnerable to tearing while playing sport. In the 1970s and 80s, a torn ACL would have ended an athlete's career. Surgical techniques from the 1990s onwards have enabled the injury to be treated successfully. One procedure used is micro-fracture surgery: small holes are drilled into the knee and from this access point micro-fractures are made in the exposed bone. These holes allow marrow to seep out and form clots which grow until they capture the torn end of the ligament, and in time this results in the ligament re-attaching to the bone.

Courtesy of the Royal College of Surgeons of Edinburgh

Dr Macintyre's X-ray film, c.1896–1909 [3]

X-rays were discovered by Wilhelm Conrad Röntgen in Germany in 1895. They allowed doctors to diagnose fractures and other injuries without surgery. This is the first X-ray cinematograph film ever taken; filmed at Glasgow Royal Infirmary and shown by Dr John Macintyre at the London Royal Society. The film shows an X-ray picture of a frog's knee joint and an X-ray of an adult. A series of these pictures enables us to see a complete cycle of the movements of the heart. The joints of the body and the movements of the digestive organs can also be seen.

Scottish Screen Archive, National Library of Scotland

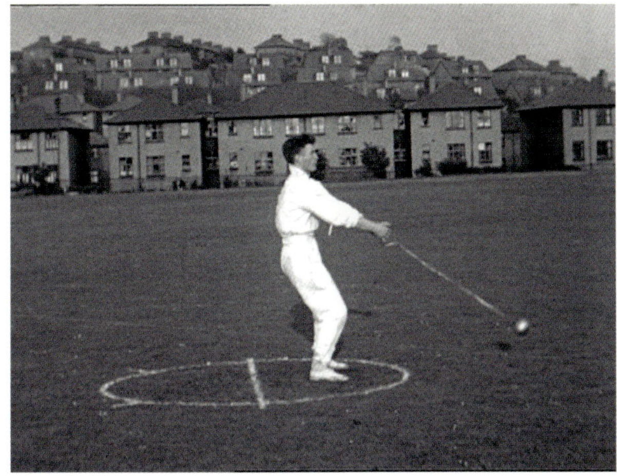

4

Film from Thomas McClurg Anderson, c.1940s–1950s [4]

Thomas McClurg Anderson (1899–1980) pioneered the development of 'ergonomics' or 'human kinetics'. He believed that 'proper training in the analysis of body movements and in physical analysis should form the essential background to physiotherapy training'. From the 1940s to the 1960s he filmed athletes of all ages and abilities, as well as clerical, domestic and factory workers. The films were used to examine and improve athletic technique as well as for research, teaching, and a programme of occupational health training at the Glasgow Physiotherapy Hospital and School.

NHS Greater Glasgow and Clyde Archives/Scottish Screen, National Library of Scotland

Underwater motion-analysis film: 'Perfect Glide'

In recent times it has been possible to analyse the performance of athletes in incredible detail as they prepare for competition. This film, highlighting the work of the Centre for Aquatic Research at the University of Edinburgh, shows sports scientists and swimming coaches using sophisticated motion-analysis computer software to improve the 'gliding' technique of elite swimmers.

Provided by The Institution of Engineering and Technology.

The Institution of Engineering and Technology is registered as a Charity in England & Wales (number 211014) and Scotland (number SC038698)

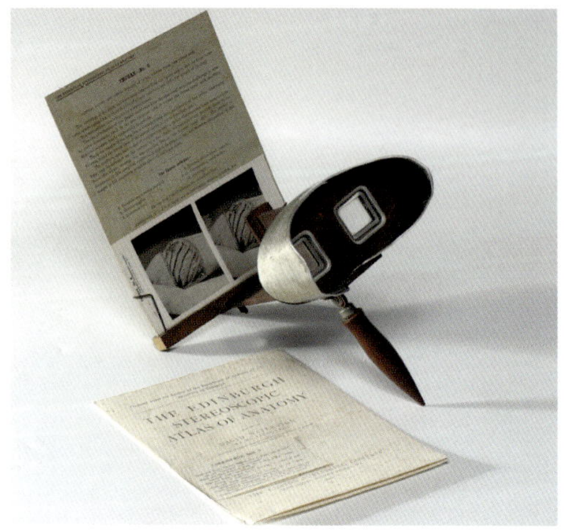

5

Thomas McClurg Anderson, *Human Kinetics and Analysing Body Movements* (1951)

Thomas McClurg Anderson was a physiotherapist in Motherwell and Glasgow, but had also been a professional boxer, athlete and sports coach. Between 1928 and 1964 he was the Principal of Glasgow Physiotherapy Hospital and School. During the 1950s he also wrote popular newspaper columns for the general public, giving advice on how to improve their sporting technique. This book shows some of the results of his filming work and research into human kinetics.

Private Collection

David Waterson, *The Edinburgh Stereoscopic Atlas of Anatomy* (London, 1906) with viewer [5]

David Waterson was a Lecturer and Senior Demonstrator in the Department of Anatomy at the University of Edinburgh. Waterson's Stereoscopic Atlas provided realistic 3D impressions of human anatomical dissections, helping students to gain important insights into the structure and spaces of the body. Stereoscopic images consist of sets of two photographs taken from very slightly different perspectives which are then viewed together through a box or hand-held viewer like this one. They contain mirrors and work rather like binoculars, giving the effect of a 3D image.

Courtesy of the Royal College of Surgeons of Edinburgh

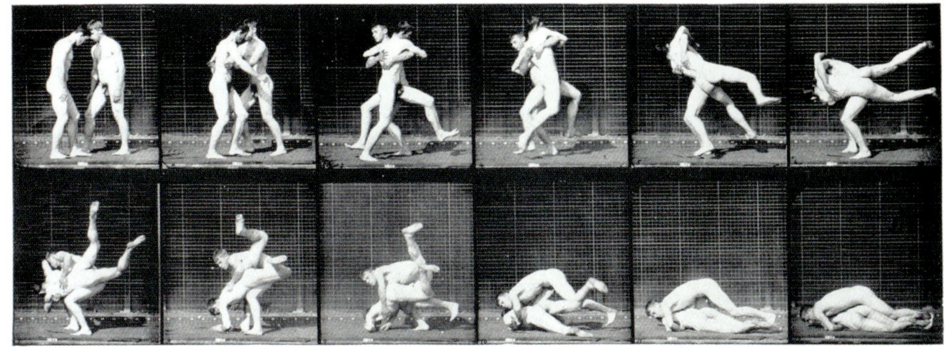

Copyright, 1887, by Eadweard Muybridge.] Series 30.

ATHLETES. WRESTLING.

6 Models 46 and 68.

For some of these phases, from the original work, see pages 215 and 217.

Étienne-Jules Marey, *On Locomotion* (Paris, 1884)

Étienne-Jules Marey (1830–1904) started his career as an assistant surgeon; he invented the 'chronophotograph' in 1888, from which modern cinematography was developed. Eadweard Muybridge (1830–1904) would later use several cameras to study the movement of animals and humans, but Marey used only one camera, and recorded movements on one photographic plate. Subjects wore black suits with metal strips or white lines as they passed in front of black backdrops.

Courtesy of the Royal College of Surgeons of Edinburgh

Athletes Wrestling from *The Human Figure in Motion,* p.75, London, 1901. Eadweard Muybridge [6]

Eadweard Muybridge (1830–1904) took more than 20,000 photographs of men, women, children and animals in movement. By using a motor clock he was able to photograph three views of the motion simultaneously. He also made moving images from his still photographs by developing a projector called a 'Zoopraxiscope'.

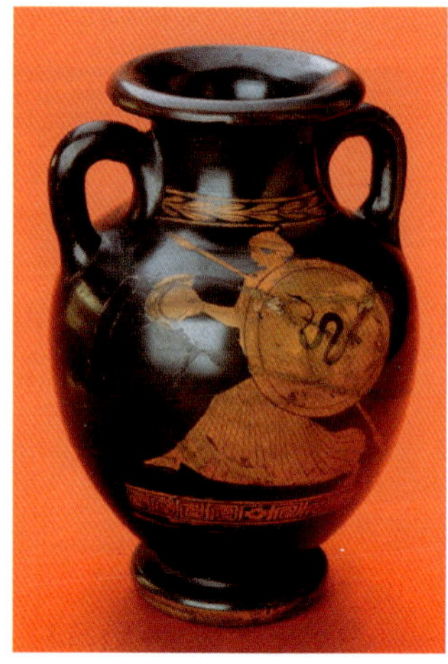
7

Amphora, 600–500 BC
[7]

The desire to accurately depict musculature and movement in the body is not a modern concept. Red-figure painting began in ancient Greek art c.530 BC. This form purposely progressed from black-figure painting so that flowing drapery as well as defined and moving figures could be shown in a more naturalistic way. In ancient Greece, physical beauty in athletes was much admired. Idealised statues such as the 'Diskoboulos' or 'discus thrower' were used to show perfect proportions and movement in sport. The discus was the first event in the pentathlon. This event exercised the whole body, so no muscles were over-developed and these athletes were seen as the most beautiful of all.

Courtesy of the University of Aberdeen

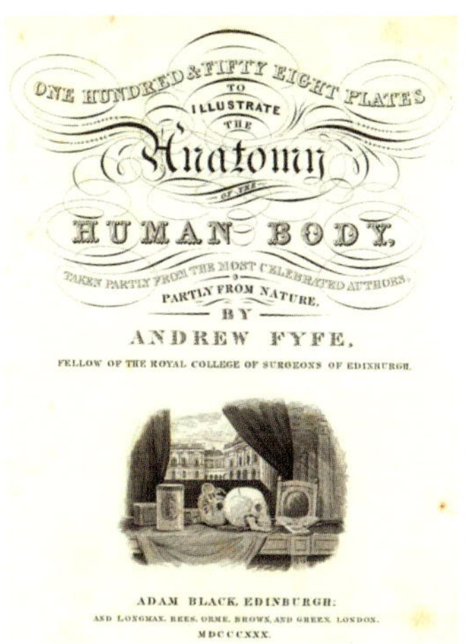

ONE HUNDRED & FIFTY EIGHT PLATES
TO
ILLUSTRATE
THE
Anatomy
OF THE
HUMAN BODY,
TAKEN PARTLY FROM THE MOST CELEBRATED AUTHORS, & PARTLY FROM NATURE.
BY
ANDREW FYFE,
FELLOW OF THE ROYAL COLLEGE OF SURGEONS OF EDINBURGH.

ADAM BLACK, EDINBURGH:
AND LONGMAN, REES, ORME, BROWN, AND GREEN, LONDON.
MDCCCXXX.

8

Andrew Fyfe, *One Hundred and Fifty Eight Plates to Illustrate the Anatomy of the Human Body* (1830) [8]

Great advances in understanding the human body were made during the 18th and 19th centuries. Andrew Fyfe (1752–1824), from Corstorphine near Edinburgh, was anatomical demonstrator to Alexander Monro (Secundus), Professor of Anatomy at the University of Edinburgh. This book was particularly popular with students attending anatomical dissection classes.

Courtesy of the Royal College of Surgeons of Edinburgh

CARING AND TREATING

The care of athletes and specialised treatment for their injuries can be traced back to ancient times. Galen (129–216 AD), who treated gladiators in the 2nd century, was probably the first 'team doctor'. Much of the more recent development of sports medicine took place in Germany from the 1890s onwards; the term 'sports physician' was first adopted in 1904. By the mid-20th century, sports medicine in the United Kingdom was dominated by the 'amateur' medic who provided assistance to the athlete during competition.

Over the past 20 years, sports medicine has been transformed from a 'hobby' interest to a discipline in its own right. In 2005, 'Sport and Exercise Medicine' was officially recognised by the United Kingdom Government as a medical specialty; The Royal College of Surgeons of Edinburgh was one of the organisations instrumental in this change.

Today, Scotland's athletes and sports teams are provided with specialist medical care before, during and after competition. Modern treatment for sports injuries requires a multidisciplinary approach which may comprise the expertise of, among others, a surgeon, soft-tissue therapist, podiatrist, sports scientist, radiologist and psychologist.

Photograph: Hanovia heat lamp, 1940s © RCSEd

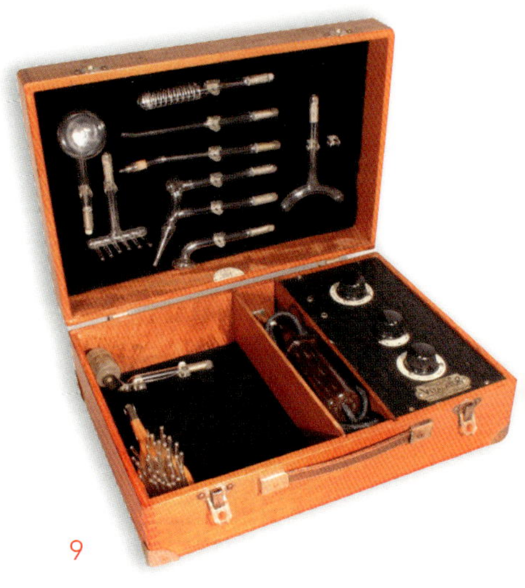

9

Allan McGraw talks about the legacy of receiving cortisone injections

McGraw (born 1939) played football for Greenock Morton and Hibernian in the 1960s. During his career he received several painkilling injections which allowed him to play while injured, but which had damaging long-term effects.

Scottish Football Museum

Craig Levein, Scotland manager, talks about his football injuries

Levein (born 1964) played 16 times for Scotland and 401 times for Heart of Midlothian. He would have played many more games if he had not suffered from a series of debilitating knee injuries throughout his career.

Scottish Football Museum

High-frequency machine ('Vitalator') c.1940 [9]

The club physiotherapist would apply the Vitalator attachments to various parts of the athlete's body in an effort to reduce pain or swelling. There is little evidence that this course of treatment was successful in treating injuries. There may, however, have been a placebo effect whereby the player believed this elaborate machine could make them better. This piece of equipment was used by Jimmy Steele (1914–1999), a masseur and physiotherapist who worked voluntarily with Celtic and Scotland for nearly 50 years.

Scottish Football Museum

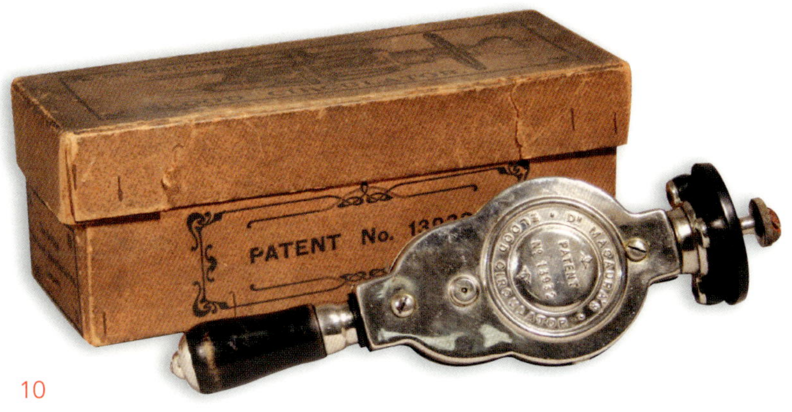

10

Hanovia heat lamp, 1940s

Heat lamps were popular treatments for sports injuries in the 1940s and 1950s. Some believed that heat therapy, using lamps like this, could aid recovery from injury by stimulating blood flow to the affected body part. Heat treatment can relieve the pain of the injury, but there is little evidence that it can accelerate healing.

Courtesy of the Royal College of Surgeons of Edinburgh

Macaura blood circulator, c.1910 [10]

In the later 19th and early 20th centuries there was a fashionable movement in Britain towards 'being your own physician'. The makers of this hand-held massager, or 'blood circulator', claimed it could cure pain, deafness, anaemia, heart disease, cramp, polio and 'women's problems'. It was invented by Gerald Joseph Macaura, who admitted that his device was useless against cancer, tuberculosis and baldness. The blood circulator was very much a therapeutic aid and proved to be not much of a remedy for any condition.

Courtesy of the Royal College of Surgeons of Edinburgh

Modern doctor's bag, 2012

The equipment used by doctors on the modern sports field consists of more than the unhygienic 'magic sponge' and bucket of cold water used in the 1950s and 1960s. Today's medical teams have equipment that is specially tailored to the needs of the athlete. Skilful on-the-spot management of injury is very important; it can accelerate recovery and, in serious cases, may save lives.

Private Collection

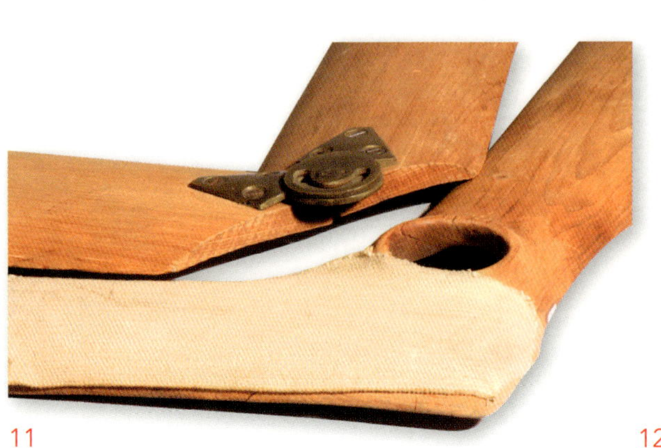

11

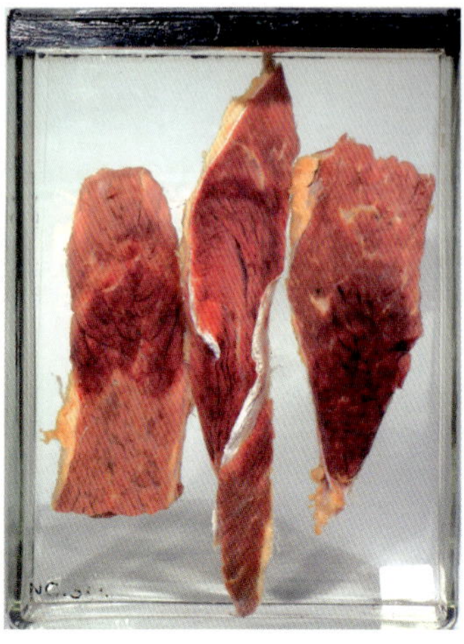

12

'Maddock's questions', c.2006

This quick and simple set of questions is used by the team doctor when treating an injured player. Asked on the field of play or on the sidelines, any incorrect response could indicate concussion and requires removal of the player from the field of play for further medical evaluation.

Scottish Rugby Union

Wooden arm and leg splint, c.1920 [11]

A hinged angled arm splint is used for holding the upper arm and forearm firmly while a fracture resets. The hinge allows the splint to be used on both arms. The left foot Cline's leg splint is used for holding the shin and ankle firmly while an ankle-break resets.

University of Glasgow, Hunterian Museum, GLAHM115371 and GLAHM115366

Muscle specimen showing bruise [12]

Bruising is one of the most common injuries suffered by players of impact sport. Eighty percent of sport and exercise injuries occur to soft tissue and do not require long-term medical treatment.

Courtesy of the Royal College of Surgeons of Edinburgh

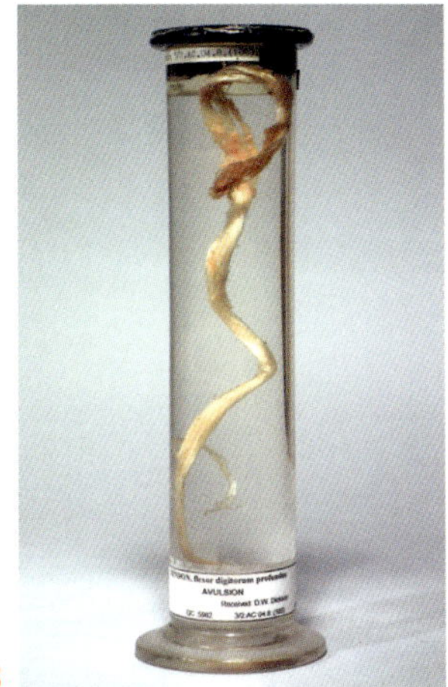

13

Knee specimen

The knee is particularly at risk of injury in many sports, especially those that involve twisting and turning (e.g. basketball) or heavy physical contact (e.g. rugby and football).

Courtesy of the Royal College of Surgeons of Edinburgh

Tendon specimen [13]

Scottish surgeon John Hunter (1728–1793) developed what is still the standard treatment for repair of a torn tendon; he operated on himself after he damaged his Achilles tendon while dancing.

Courtesy of the Royal College of Surgeons of Edinburgh

Foot specimen

Injuries to the foot and ankle are among the most common in sport. Injuries usually occur as a result of a direct blow, a twisting injury, or overuse.

Courtesy of the Royal College of Surgeons of Edinburgh

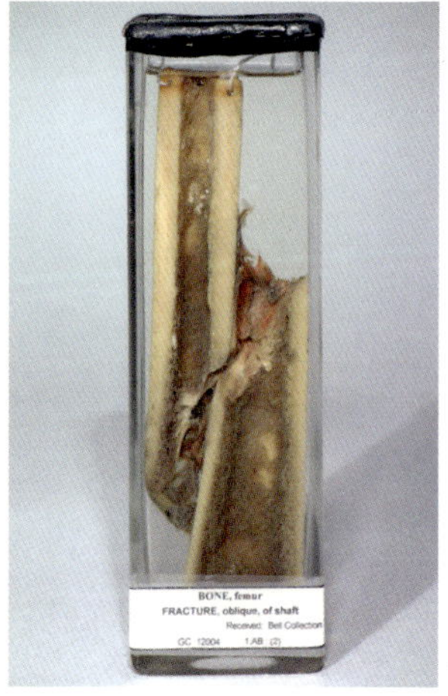

14

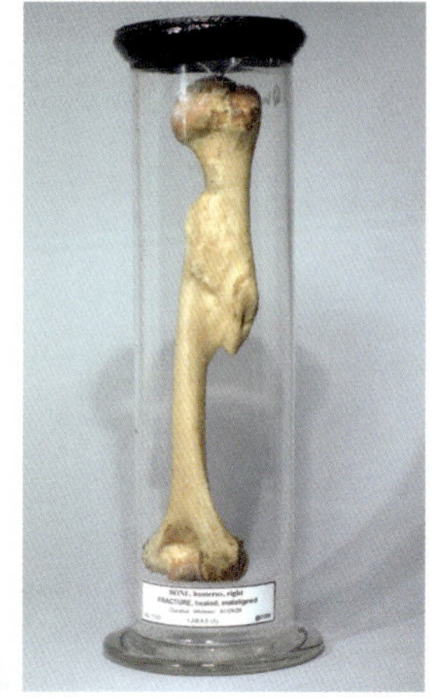

15

Femur fracture [14]

As diagnoses have improved, so has the surgical treatment of sports injuries. A 'fracture' is no longer just a 'fracture' but rather one of a range of breaks that occur for different reasons and which take different forms. Similar injuries can be treated in different ways depending on which sport the athlete plays. The swimmer's damaged ankle which needs great flexibility will be treated differently from a runner, where more intense (but limited) ankle movement is required.

Courtesy of the Royal College of Surgeons of Edinburgh, GC12004

Humerus fracture [15]

Most broken bones heal successfully once they have been correctly aligned and immobilised. However, this is an example of what can happen if the bone is not set appropriately.

Courtesy of the Royal College of Surgeons of Edinburgh, GC7703

Heart specimen showing a rupture of the left ventricle

The left ventricle is the heart's main pumping chamber. With many hours of training an athlete can develop a powerful left ventricle and slower resting heart rate. These changes are sometimes called 'athletic heart syndrome' and are usually harmless. This syndrome does, however, look similar in several tests to an inherited enlargement of heart muscle, hypertrophic cardiomyopathy, which can lead to heart weakness. A small number of sudden deaths of athletes, who were apparently fit with no history of heart problems, have been caused by cardiomyopathy.

Courtesy of the Royal College of Surgeons of Edinburgh

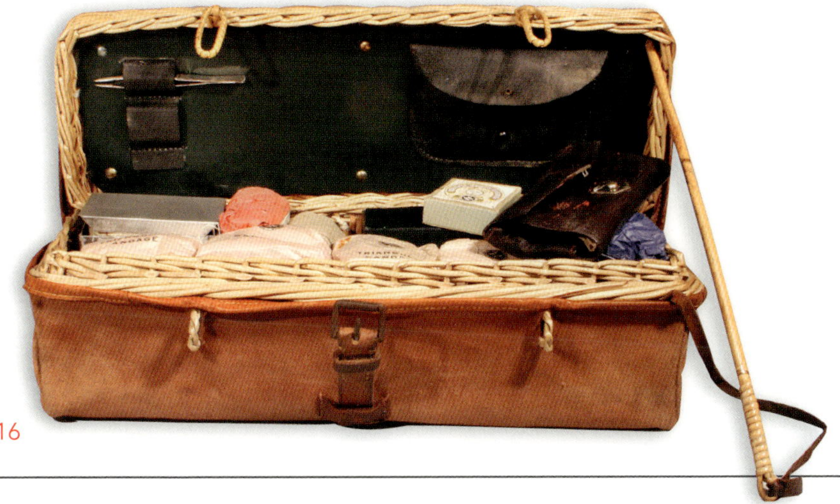

16

Hoffman single-bar external fixation

This is one way of holding the broken bone in the appropriate position as it heals. External fixators can be made of metal or carbon fibre, and have steel pins that pass into the bone directly through the skin.

Courtesy of the Royal College of Surgeons of Edinburgh

First-Aid kit, St John Ambulance Association, c.1950s [16]

Established in 1877, the St John Ambulance Association provided first-aid training to the public. Volunteers from this organisation have also attended thousands of events, including sports meetings, where they cared for the sick and injured. This bag contains numerous items, including various bandages and smelling salts.

Courtesy of the Royal College of Surgeons of Edinburgh

Jimmy Steele's homemade treatment table

Jimmy Steele (1914–1999), universally known as 'Steelie', was a masseur and physiotherapist who worked voluntarily with Celtic and Scotland for nearly 50 years. Before working with footballers he worked with the boxer Freddie Mills. 'Steelie' invented several machines to treat the footballers in his care. This treatment table was one of these contraptions and included adjustable supports, a bearskin rug and light bulbs to be used for heat treatment.

Scottish Football Museum

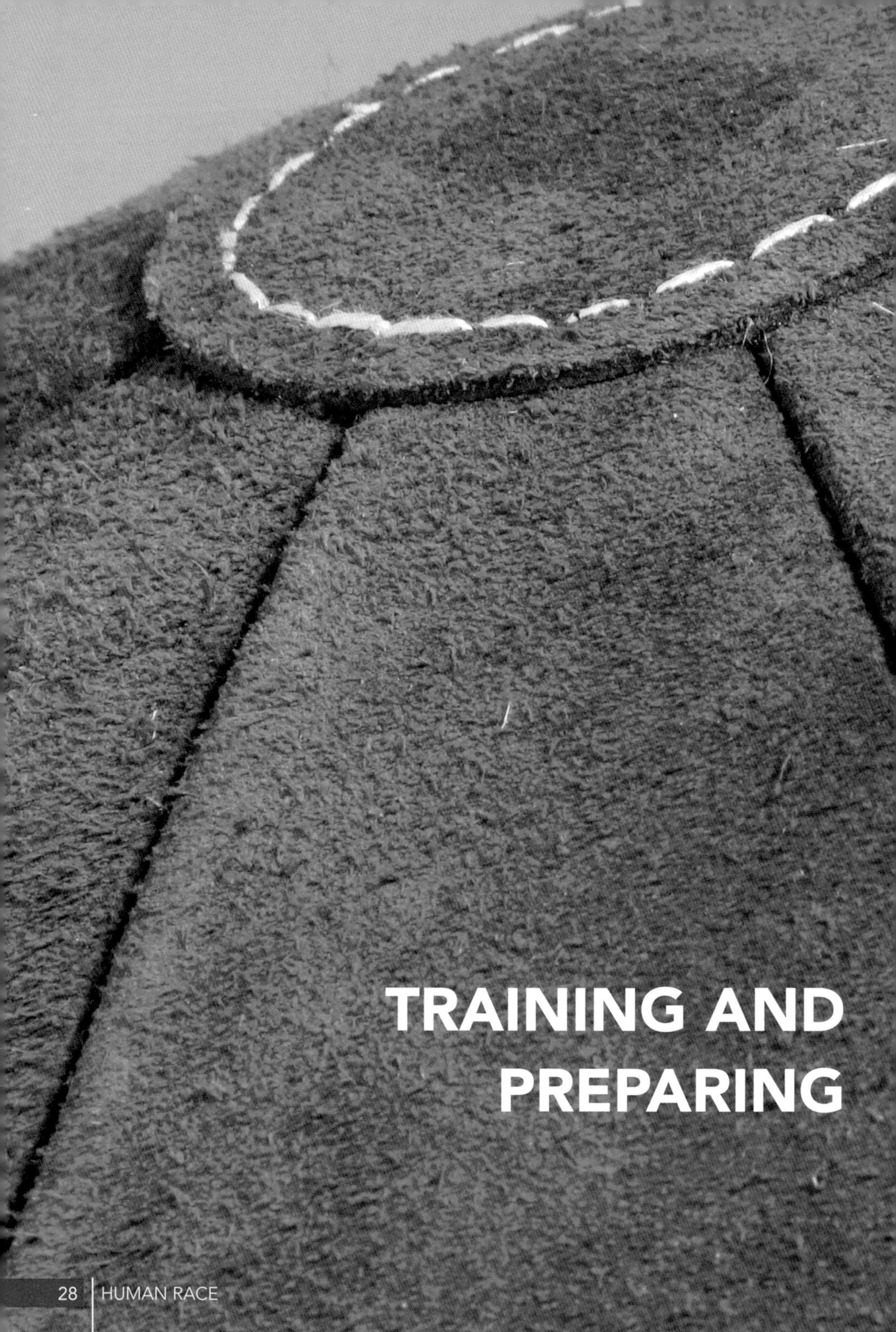

TRAINING AND PREPARING

Training is the process of straining the physiological systems of the body to condition it for competition. Training athletes means systematically and progressively increasing the strain that the athletes are put under for their body to adapt and become stronger, faster and fitter.

Training specifically for sport emerged in the middle of the 18th century. Popular sports of the time such as pedestrianism (competitive walking), prize fighting (boxing) and rowing were linked to gambling. Therefore, training and coaching took place to better the chances of sporting (and therefore financial) success. Early coaches were often farmers who had a background in training racehorses.

Most early training was aimed at achieving the balance of the body's four 'humours': earth, fire, water, air (each was associated with black bile, yellow bile, phlegm and blood). The 18th-century sports trainer believed these impediments had to be removed through a combination of diet, exercise and medication. The body was seen as a fixed and stable machine with limited energy levels, which applied to mental and physical activity.

Significant changes to ideas about sports training and diet took place in the middle of the 19th century. Pioneering Scots such as Archibald MacLaren from Alloa were part of a European-wide emergence of modern-day 'scientific training'. MacLaren was among the first to dismiss the traditional methods of 'purging', 'physicking', 'forced sweating' and 'restriction of fluids' in favour of the regulation of exercise and a varied diet.

Photograph: Detail of medicine ball

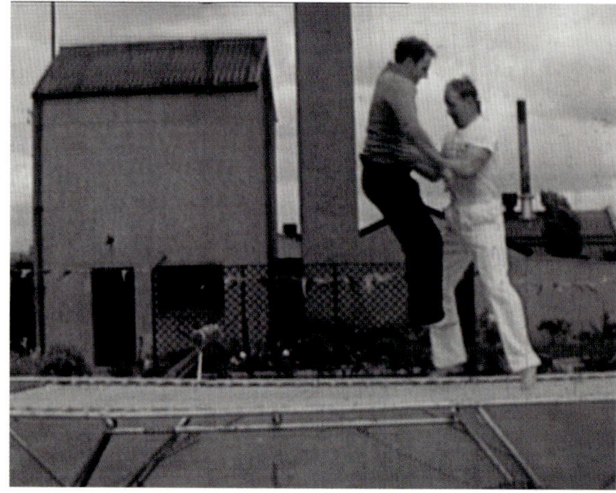

17

'Jumping for Joy', c.1958 [17]

This semi-instructional film shows how the trampoline was used for general sports training but also the rehabilitation of injured miners. Made with the co-operation of the Scottish Council for Physical Recreation, it was filmed at Inverclyde National Centre, the Miners Rehabilitation Centre in Bellshill, and at St Aidan's School, Bridgeton, Glasgow.

Scottish Screen Archive, National Library of Scotland

Medicine ball

The medicine ball is one of the earliest forms of strength and conditioning training. In ancient Greece, Hippocrates is known to have filled animal skins with sand for the rehabilitation of his patients.

Courtesy of the Royal College of Surgeons of Edinburgh

Archibald MacLaren, *Training in Theory and Practice* (1866)

Significant changes to ideas about sports training and diet took place from the middle of the 19th century. Archibald MacLaren (1819–1894) from Alloa was part of a European-wide emergence of modern-day 'scientific training'. MacLaren studied gymnastics and medicine in Paris and later trained rowers at Oxford University. In 1857, MacLaren opened his gymnasium at Oxford, where he started to test his methods on small numbers of British Army soldiers. He was the author of several books on physical education, including this training manual.

MacLaren dismissed traditional practices of 'purging' and promoted instead regulation of exercise and a varied diet which included more vegetables, eggs, meat and farinaceous (starchy) foods. His system of physical training was adopted by the British Army and British public schools in the later 19th century.

Courtesy of the National Library of Scotland

Alex Main talks about football training at Inverness in the 1950s.

Scottish Football Museum

Whip belonging to Captain Robert Barclay Allardice, c.1820s

Captain Robert Barclay Allardice (1779–1854), otherwise known as the 'celebrated pedestrian', was born at Ury House, near Stonehaven in Aberdeenshire. He was renowned as a competitive walker, and his most challenging feat was a bet to walk 1,000 miles in 1,000 consecutive hours, which he completed to the astonishment of many in 1807. Robert Barclay Allardice wrote the pamphlet *Training for Pedestrianism and Boxing* (1816), and promoted his own training regimen and diet. He was also the sponsor and trainer of Tom Cribb, bare-knuckle boxing champion of the world in 1807 and 1809.

Courtesy of the University of Aberdeen

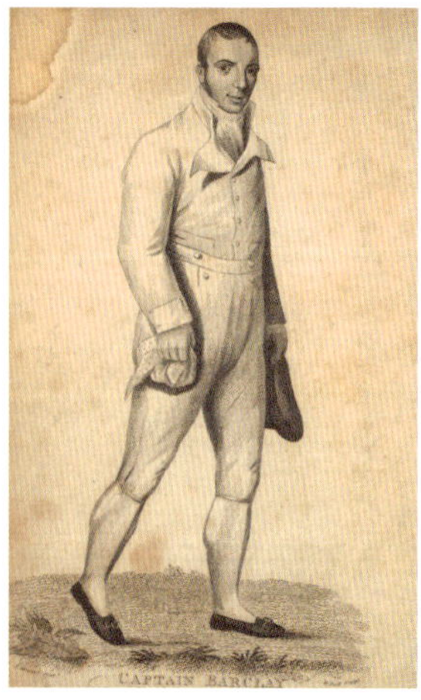

18

Walter Thom, *Pedestrianism* (1813) [18]

This is often credited as the first modern (post-Renaissance) book specifically devoted to athletes and training. Walter Thom, from Aberdeen, wrote in great detail about Captain Robert Barclay Allardice's sporting achievements and his punishing training and dietary regimen.

Courtesy of the National Library of Scotland

Sir John Sinclair, '*The Code of Health and Longevity*' (Edinburgh, Arch. Constable and Co, 1807)

Sir John Sinclair (1754–1835) from Thurso is remembered primarily as an agricultural improver, but he wrote prolifically on many issues, including finance and statistics. In 1806 he carried out the first analysis of sports training in Great Britain. In particular, Sinclair discussed training for pedestrianism (competitive walking) and pugilism (boxing). Sinclair found the main objective of sports training was to develop good 'wind' (stamina). This was achieved with a diet of undercooked red meat, dry bread and old beer. Sinclair's enquiries found that for most training practices (largely consisting of walking and running exercises) there was little difference between the training of animals such as horses and greyhounds and the training of boxers and pedestrians.

Courtesy of the National Library of Scotland

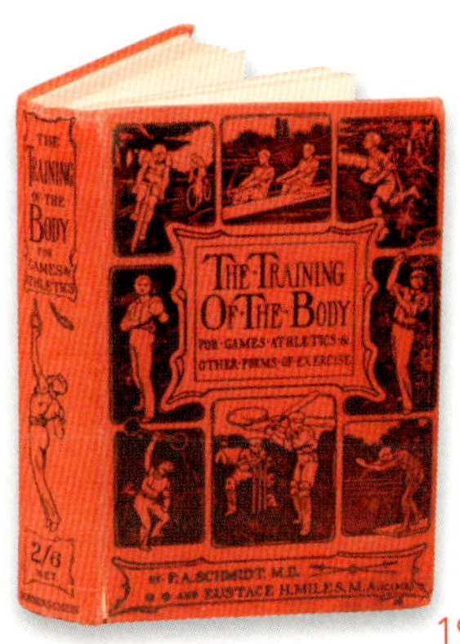

19

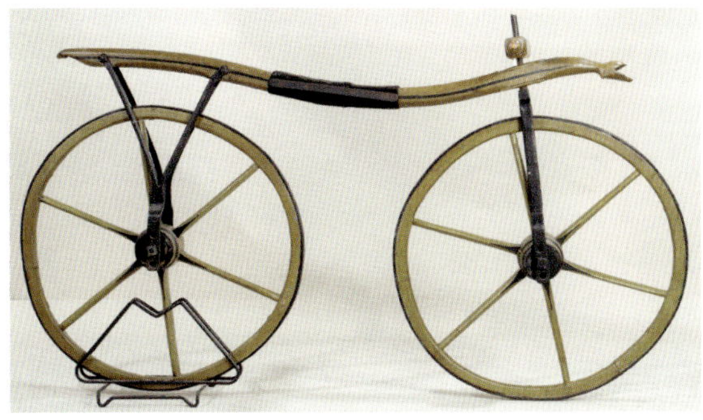

20

'Training of the Body' (1901) [19]

By the end of the Victorian period there was a large market in manuals and books offering training and medical advice relating to sport. These books were aimed at a literate 'gentlemanly sportsman' who had plenty of money to spare.

Private collection

'Hobby horse', c.1820s [20]

This was a popular and fashionable method of transport in the time of Captain Robert Barclay Allardice. Designed by Karl Drais (1785–1851), this 'Laufmachine' was also known as a 'running machine' or 'velocipede', 'draisine' or 'dandy horse'. The dandy horse (so-called because they were owned by the fashionable 'dandies' of the time) was propelled forward by the rider by pushing his/her feet along the ground.

Courtesy of Glasgow Museums

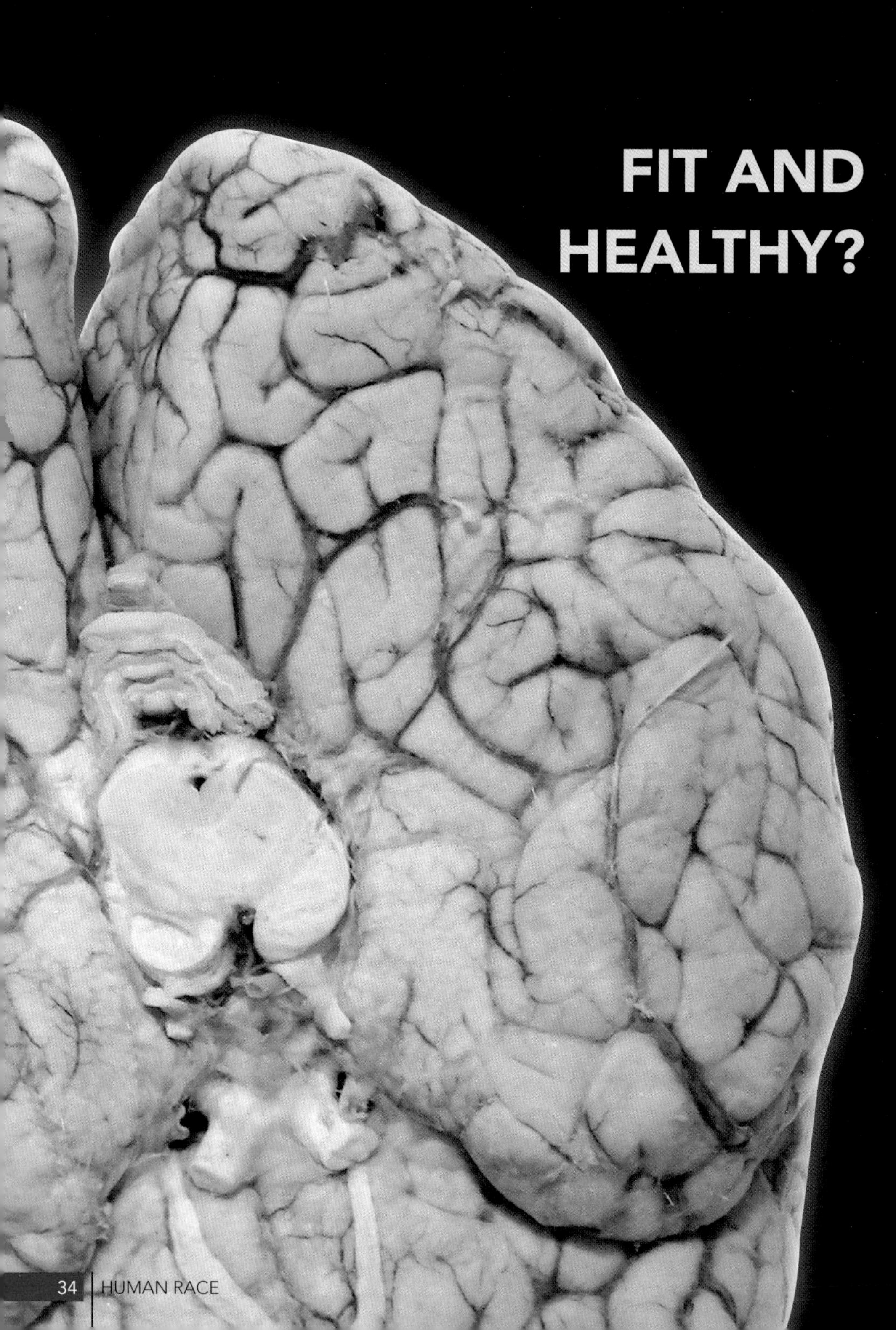

FIT AND HEALTHY?

'If we could give every individual the right amount of nourishment and exercise; not too little and not too much, we would have found the safest way to health.'

Hippocrates (c.460–377 BC)

The link between exercise and wellbeing has been acknowledged since ancient times. In the 5th century BC, therapeutic exercise was pioneered by the Greek physician Herodicus as a way to maintain good health. We now know that playing sport and exercising can help strengthen muscles, joints and bones; improve suppleness, breathing and circulation; protect against disease; lower stress and anxiety levels; and help to combat depression.

There have been numerous campaigns in Scotland devised to promote the benefits of physical activity to the wider population. In the 1930s the National Fitness Council for Scotland tried to stimulate public interest in sport and exercise through a series of films which were shown at the Glasgow Empire Exhibition of 1938. Subsequent campaigns, with messages about improving diet and increasing physical activity, have been used to try to improve Scotland's poor public health record.

For some sportsmen and women professional sport can actually be unhealthy in the longer term. Elite athletes are put under huge physical and psychological stresses and strains during their careers, which can sometimes have a negative cumulative effect, often becoming obvious only if they stop competing.

21

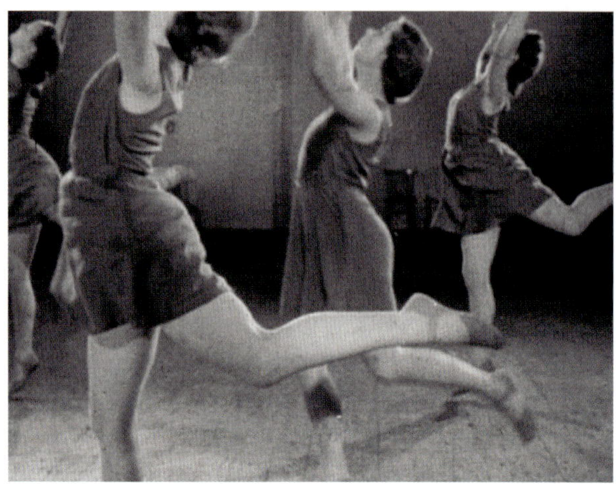

'Scotland for Fitness', 1938

This film was part of a campaign to improve the fitness of the Scottish population. It was one of a group of seven films made for the 1938 Empire Exhibition under the supervision of John Grierson (1898–1972). Grierson was the founding father of documentary film-making; he coined the phrase 'documentary', which he described as 'the imaginative creation of reality'.

Scottish Screen, National Library of Scotland

'4 and 20 Fit Girls', 1942 [21]

This film demonstrates the emphasis placed on traditional roles in wartime Britain. Men's fitness was defined by a militaristic structure, focusing on strength and power. However, this film shows women's fitness concentrating on movement, co-ordination and gentle exercise. It not only encourages women to be fit, it also offers a prescriptive view of a woman's reason to exercise, with references to aspirations of 'beauty', being fit for 'housework' and 'washing up'.

Scottish Screen, National Library of Scotland

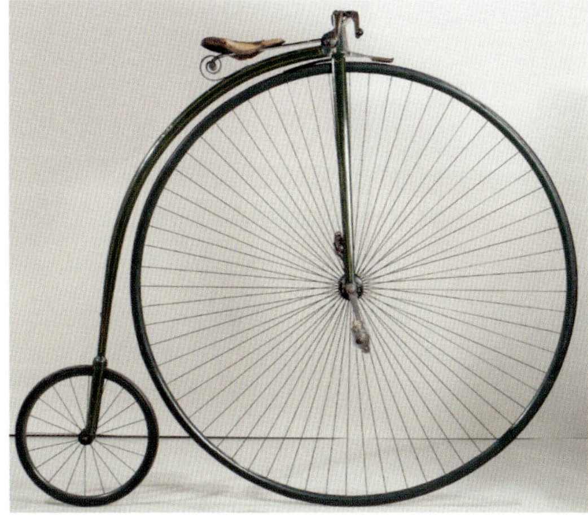
22

Howe 'Spider' bicycle, c.1885 [22]

Made by Howe Cycles in Bridgeton, Glasgow, this bicycle was known as a 'high' cycle, or later as the 'Penny Farthing'. This was one of 12 models produced by the company, which exported widely to Europe and had sales offices in Paris and Moscow. The growth in the popularity of the bicycle soon led to Scotland becoming a destination for tourists looking for a sporting holiday. One of the first sporting tourists was C.B. Reade, a retired English sea captain who wrote under the name 'Nauticus'. He toured the Highlands on a tricycle in 1881, writing about his experiences. He travelled 30–40 miles a day, for 69 days. 'Nauticus' compared the healthy nature of his tour with tourists who travelled by train: 'The cyclist, instead of being tied down to certain lines of route and halting places, is like the bee, free to settle where he pleases, and having taken the essence out of one place, can flit on to the next… All this, with the pure, bracing air and the exhilarating exercise, combine to give both mind and body healthy recreation.'

Courtesy of Glasgow Museums

Acts of Parliament banning football

The government in Scotland has not always encouraged the people to play the sports they enjoy most. In 1457, Scotland's parliament banned golf and football because it took them away from archery practice, which was necessary in times of war.

Private Collection

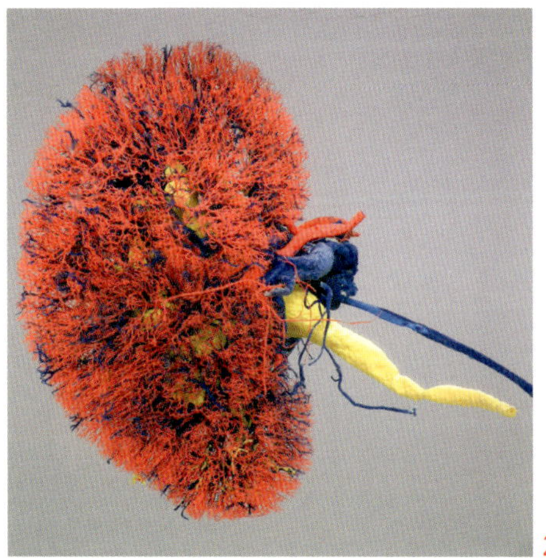

23

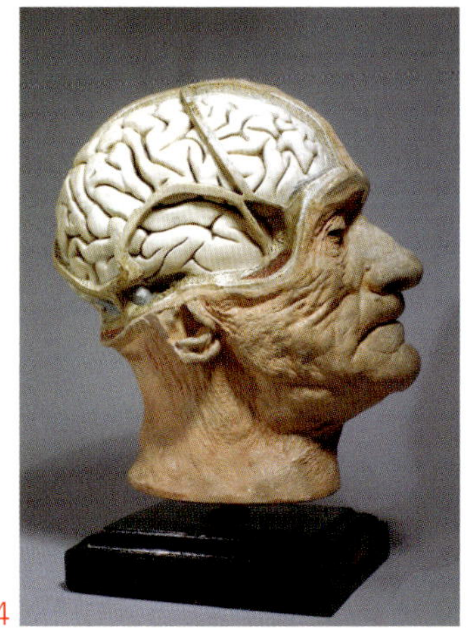

24

Kidney specimen [23]

Damage to the kidney can happen in sports such as boxing, where blunt force is used. This cast of the left kidney shows the delicate internal structure of the organ.

Courtesy of the Royal College of Surgeons of Edinburgh

Model of the head, cast from death, showing the normal internal structure of the brain [24]

Courtesy of the Royal College of Surgeons of Edinburgh

Specimens of skull and brain

The brain is protected within the skull and is enveloped within three layers (membranes) known as the 'meninges'. The outer layer is the 'dura mater'; it is stuck firmly to the inside of the skull. Arteries lie between the dura mater and the skull. A blow to the head can cause a skull fracture that can tear one of these arteries, causing it to bleed. As the blood collects it will peel the dura mater away from the inside of the skull. This pushes into the brain and, as the pressure grows, the person becomes unconscious. If left untreated, the

25

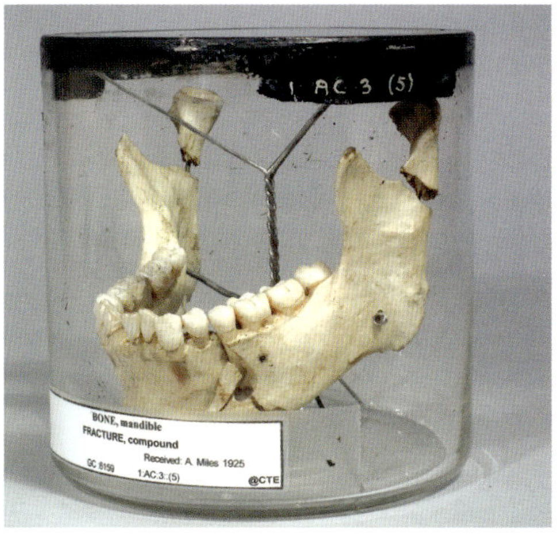

brain will eventually be compressed until the vital functions of breathing and heart control fail.

The long-term effects of some sports on the body are beginning to be fully understood. Repetitive injuries to the brain can occur in football, American football, boxing and other impact sports. This accumulative damage to the brain was formerly known as dementia pugilistica (punch-drunk syndrome) and is now known as chronic traumatic encephalopathy (CTE).

Courtesy of the Royal College of Surgeons of Edinburgh

Compound fracture of the mandible (lower jaw) [25]

Common sports injuries to the face and scalp tend to be soft-tissue bruises (contusions) and cuts (lacerations). These injuries can sometimes be complicated by injuries to the underlying bones.

Courtesy of the Royal College of Surgeons of Edinburgh

Vertebrae specimen

Most elite sportsmen and women will suffer from a back injury at some point in their career. Some injuries to the back, such as fractures of the vertebrae, may require surgery because they can cause damage to the rest of the spinal cord.

Courtesy of the Royal College of Surgeons of Edinburgh

PUSHING LIMITS AND BREAKING BOUNDARIES

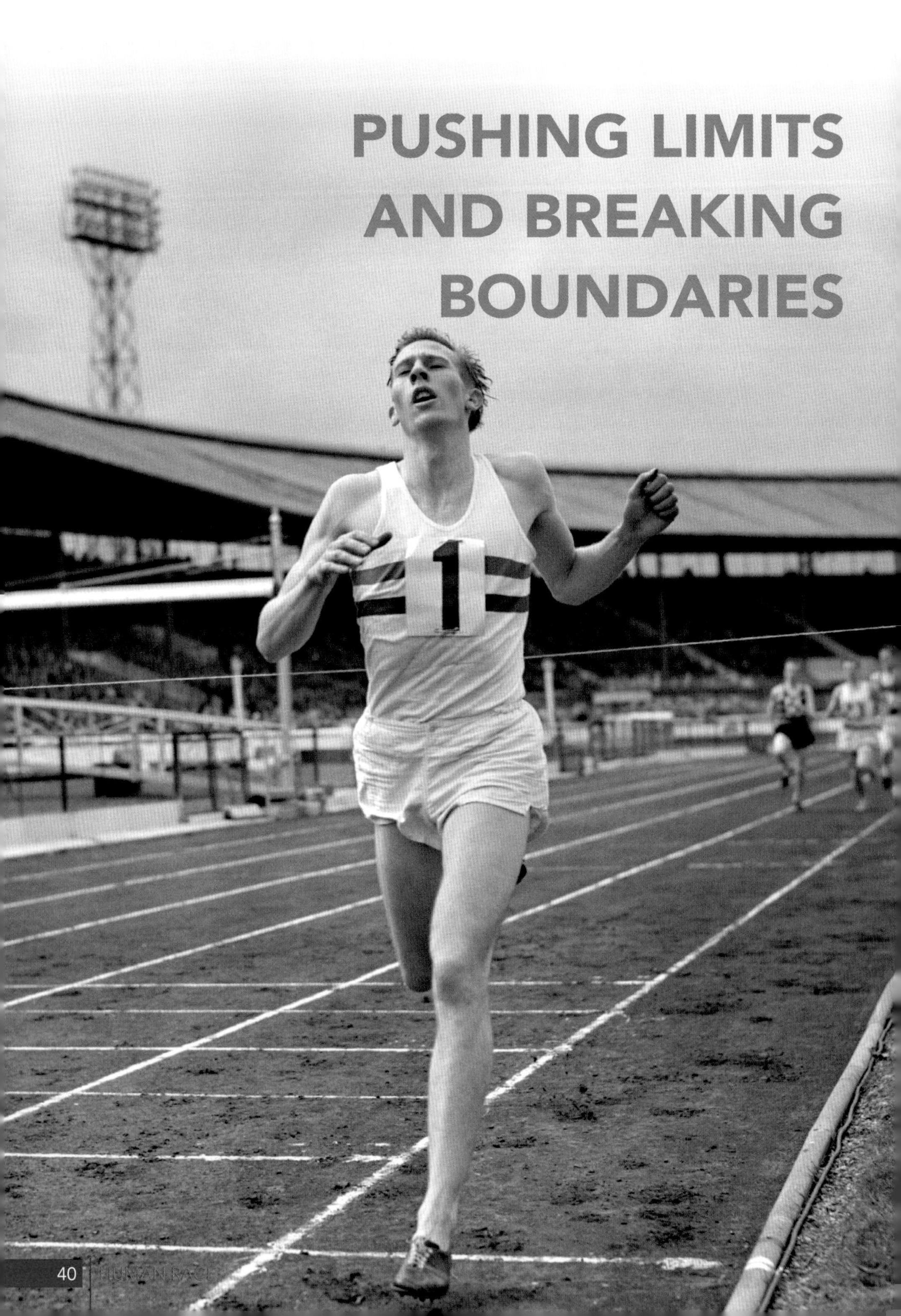

'Doctors and scientists said that breaking the four-minute mile was impossible, that one would die in the attempt. Thus, when I got up from the track after collapsing at the finish line, I figured I was dead.'

Sir Roger Bannister CBE (born 1929)

The physical limits of the human body have changed over time. Athletic feats that were once viewed as impossible, such as running a mile in less than 4 minutes or 100 metres in less than 10 seconds, are now routinely achieved.

As the human body has evolved, we have progressively increased our understanding of human physiology, training, and the preparation required for competing at an elite level. However, many observers increasingly believe we are reaching a plateau in what the human body can physically accomplish in sport, and that any future improvements in sports performance will have to rely on technological and biomechanical advances.

For as long as sporting competition has taken place, athletes have sought to gain advantage over their competitors and changes to the technology and materials used in sport have continually taken place over the years. Although these changes are governed by specific regulations in sports such as swimming and golf, the concept of what constitutes an unfair advantage to the competitor is a continually shifting area of debate.

For some competitors, seeking an advantage has meant using performance enhancing drugs. Since the 1960s, 'doping' in sport has been strictly controlled, but drugs continue to be used by elite athletes and the subject remains controversial.

Photograph: Roger Bannister

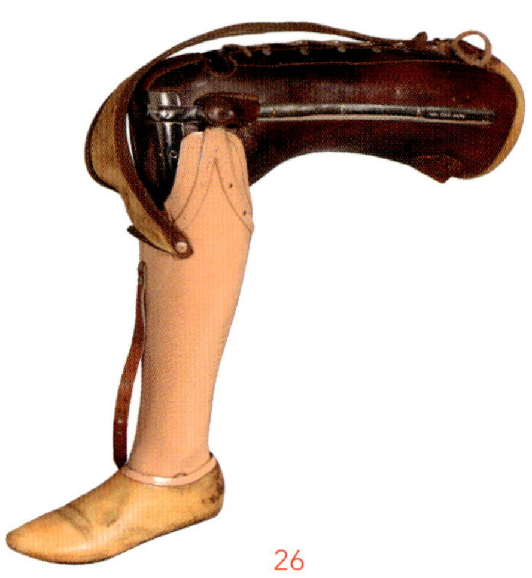

Prosthetic limb by Kellie of Dundee [26]

Modern prosthesis, SPEEAD project, 2011

There have been dramatic advances in the development of prostheses in the past century. Rapid improvements to their design and ease of use were made after the First World War (1914–1918), but more significantly after the Second World War (1939–1945), in which many soldiers lost limbs in conflict.

Courtesy of the Royal College of Surgeons of Edinburgh

Developments in biomechanics have allowed many amputees to take part in exercise and enjoy their favourite sports. The materials used to make prostheses have changed from woods and metals to plastics and polymers. The modern prosthetic is increasingly efficient, performs better in competition, and is more comfortable for the athlete to wear. Scotland is a leader in this area, and has had a key role in these developments. This prosthetic is from the Sports Prosthetics for Elite and Everyday Athletes with a Disability (SPEEAD project) at the University of Strathclyde.

University of Strathclyde

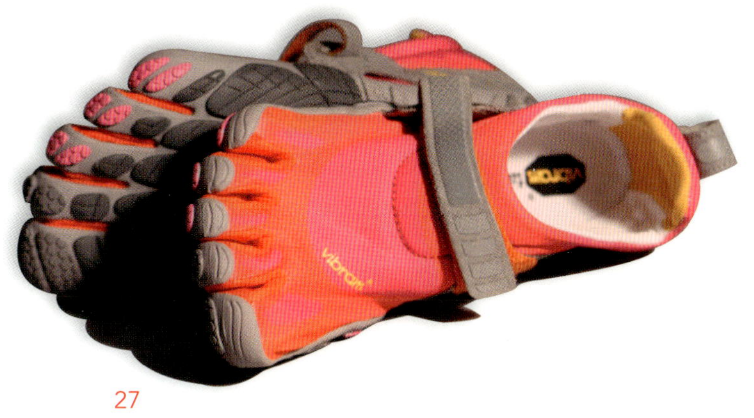

27

The Bartlett Tendon

Brian Bartlett, a professional downhill mountain biker from the USA, was the inventor of the Bartlett Tendon. The Bartlett Tendon allows above-the-knee amputees to cycle and can also be used for other sports such as skiing, waterskiing and snowboarding. The Bartlett Tendon is a fluid mechanical device combined with an artificial muscle or tendon to provide the wearer with the 'human' feeling of a real limb.

Courtesy of Brian Bartlett

Vibram 'Five Fingers' running shoes [27]

According to the manufacturers, the thin, flexible sole and individual 'toe pockets' help strengthen and stretch muscles in the feet, improving balance and agility. The shoe replicates being barefoot, and is said to allow for the natural biomechanics of the foot to work.

Private Collection

Bronze-Age archer's wrist guards, 600–2400 BC

These wrist guards, an early form of protection used during archery, were found in a stone-lined pit (known as a cist) on a farm at Newlands, Oyne, in Aberdeenshire in 1935. During the Bronze Age, a new style of individual burial appeared. The body was interred in a cist or, if cremated, in an urn. Usually objects such as beakers or food vessels and other artefacts relating to the status of the person (such as these wrist guards) accompanied the body.

Courtesy of the University of Aberdeen

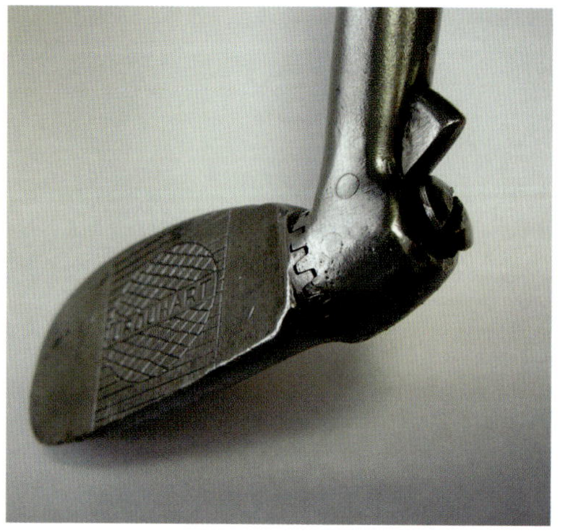

28

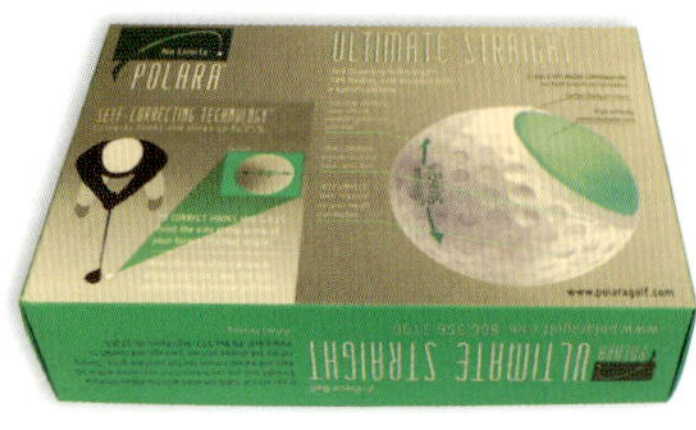

29

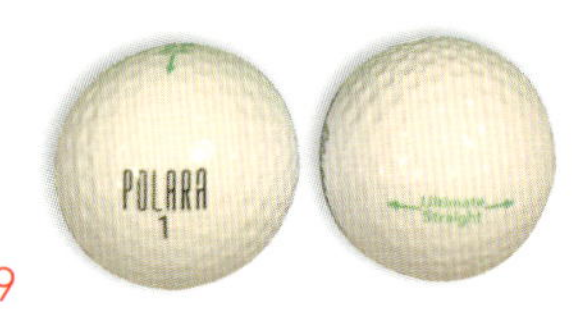

Urquhart adjustable iron golf club, c.1900 [28]

Between 1892 and 1902, Robert Urquhart of Edinburgh sought to make the perfect adjustable golf club. Golfers could change the loft of the clubface, enabling them to play various shots (including putting) with a single club. Urquhart's model was the most successful, but adjustable clubs were not widely popular. Many golfers felt convenience came at the expense of balance, feel and performance. In 1909, the Rules of Golf Committee of The Royal and Ancient Golf Club of St Andrews began legislating on club design for the first time. It wished to limit the 'departure from the traditional and accepted form and make of golf clubs'. The Committee ruled that clubs should consist of a head which did not contain mechanical or adjustable parts. Clubs such as the Urquhart were therefore banned.

The British Golf Museum

Polara golf ball [29]

This ball has 'self-correcting technology'. The combination of deep and shallow dimples on the surface of the ball allows it to 'self-adjust' during flight, reducing hooks and slices on the golf course by up to 75%. The golfing authorities banned the use of this 'aerodynamic asymmetrical ball' in competitive golf in 1981.

Private Collection

Speedo LZR swimsuit

This swimsuit has a 'core stabiliser' and polyurethane panels which help position the swimmer higher in the water than was previously the case with a regular swimsuit. An integrated corset makes it up to 70-times tighter than other swimwear. The fabric was invented to cut the drag in the water and make the athlete more hydrodynamic. Swimmers move more easily through the water, so they economise on the oxygen that they use by 5%. These suits were deemed to be 'performance-enhancing' by swimming authorities, and were banned from being used in competitive swimming on 1 January 2010. Speedo was founded by Alexander MacRae (c.1888–1938). MacRae was from the Kyle of Lochalsh but emigrated to Australia in 1910 and established MacRae Hosiery Manufacturers. The company was awarded a contract to produce socks for the Australian Army, and the profits allowed the company to expand to produce swimwear. In 1928, the 'Speedo' name was introduced and the company unveiled a one-piece cotton 'Racer-back' costume. This was one of the first pieces of specifically designed sportswear for athletes. The new design allowed greater freedom of movement and enabled swimmers to swim faster, but the exposed arms and shoulders caused controversy.

Private Collection

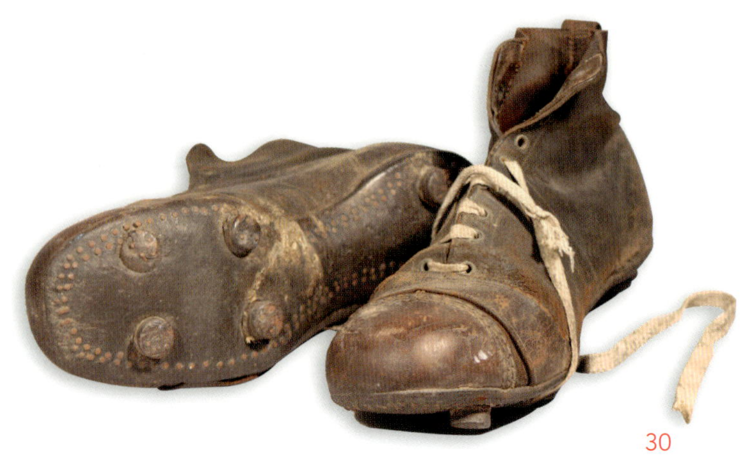

Football boots, c.1940s [30]

Football boots in the 1940s were made from heavy leather. They supported the ankle of the player but would have been liable to cause injury to others. Like the footballs of the time they also absorbed moisture and got very heavy in wet conditions.

Scottish Football Museum

Puma v1.11 football boots, 2012

Football boots have changed dramatically in appearance over the last 20 years. These boots are made from synthetic leather and have a carbon-fibre sole, they weigh only 232g. Sometimes changes to the design of sports equipment are not beneficial; some football-club doctors attribute an increase in metatarsal injuries to the growth in popularity of bladed football boots like these.

Private Collection

Football, c.1940s

On wet days, a leather football like this would soak up large amounts of water. After 90 minutes, the ball could often weigh 900g; more than twice its original weight.

Scottish Football Museum

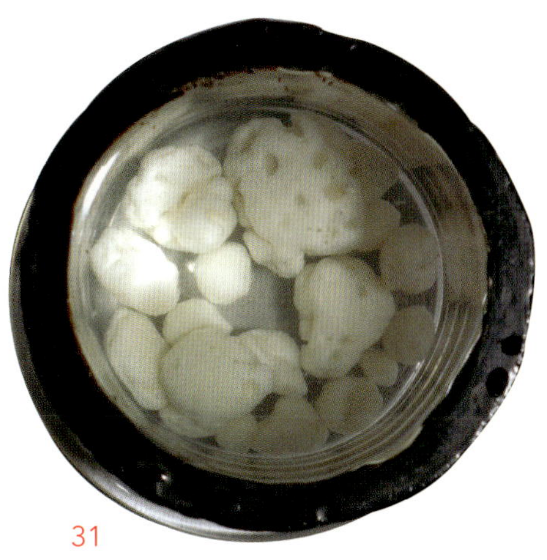

31

Adidas football, UEFA European Championships, 2012

Adidas claim that this 'Tango 12' football is the most extensively tested ball in history. Part of the testing process involved a 'Robi-Leg', a robotic leg with a football on it that simulates the impact of a human foot on a football at speeds of up to 100 miles per hour.

Private Collection

Keyhole surgery instruments

Laparoscopic ('keyhole') surgery or minimally invasive surgery was pioneered in Dundee by Professor Sir Alfred Cuschieri (born 1938). This type of procedure reduces the level of intervention needed and decreases post-operative pain and recovery times. The benefit for the athlete is seen by quicker rehabilitation and faster return to competition.

Courtesy of the Royal College of Surgeons of Edinburgh

Loose bodies in knee [31]

Athletes often require a 'clean up' of their knee. Keyhole surgery is frequently used to undertake procedures such as the removal of loose bodies.

Courtesy of the Royal College of Surgeons of Edinburgh

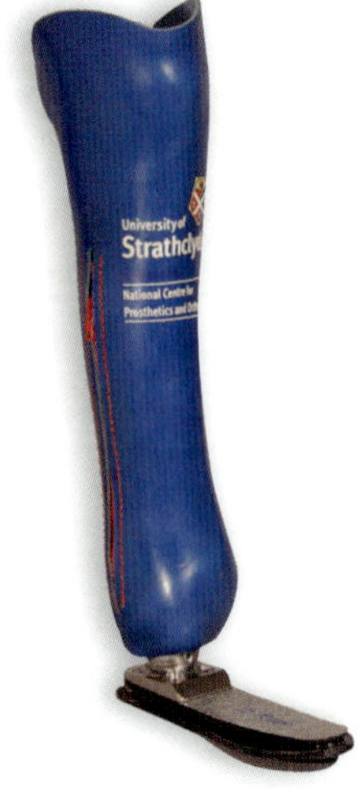

32

Syme Flex Foot [32]

In 1843, Sir James Syme (1799–1870) from Edinburgh pioneered amputation of the ankle joint. One of the world's leading prosthetic manufacturers now makes foot prostheses which are named the 'Syme'.

University of Strathclyde/ National Centre for Prosthetics and Orthotics

James Syme, cast of his hand with scalpel

James Syme, the 'Napoleon of Surgery', carried out the first hip amputation in Scotland, but was known primarily for his ankle–joint amputation.

Courtesy of the Royal College of Surgeons of Edinburgh

Menisectomy knives

Orthopaedics developed as a recognised specialty in the first half of the 20th century. One of the first orthopaedic surgeons in Scotland was Professor Ian Smillie (1907–1992), who became a world authority on knee surgery. Injury to the knee can often result in damage to the meniscus; Smillie pioneered the procedure which removed the damaged meniscus from the knee joint. He designed these special knives and other surgical tools to conduct the procedure effectively.

University of Dundee Museum Services, Tayside Medical History Museum, DUNUC4376

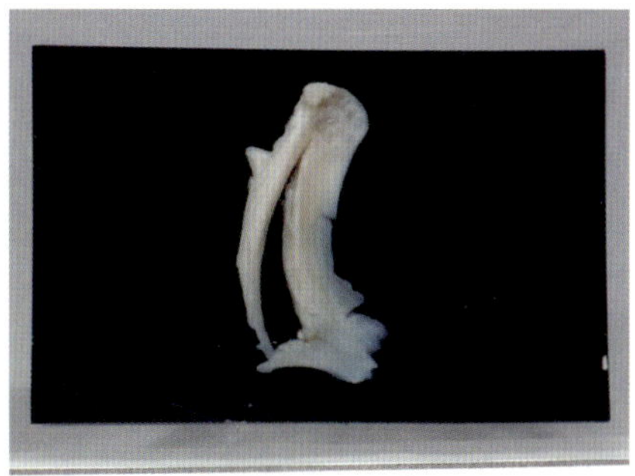

JOINT, knee, meniscus
TEAR, longitudinal
Received: D.S. Middleton

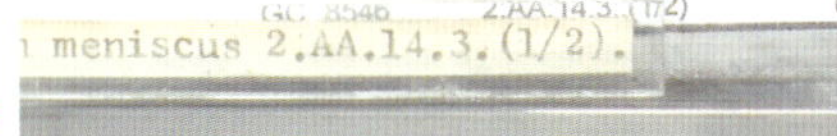

33

Ian Smillie, *'Injuries of the Knee Joint'* (1946)

This is one of the earliest modern textbooks that directly made a link between injuries and playing sport. Professor Smillie was appointed surgeon in charge of the Orthopaedic Service for Eastern Scotland on the formation of the NHS in 1948. He established orthopaedic clinics in Dundee, and became the first holder of the Chair of Orthopaedic Surgery at the University of St Andrews.

University of Dundee Museum Services, Tayside Medical History Museum

Meniscus specimen [33]

Professor Ian Smillie pioneered the procedure which removed the damaged meniscus from the knee joint. Today, 'keyhole surgery' is favoured because the damaged tissue is removed rather than the entire meniscus.

Courtesy of the Royal College of Surgeons of Edinburgh

WADA list and examples of banned substances

For centuries, athletes have tried to gain competitive advantage by supplementing their bodies with different substances. To moderate drug use in sport, the International Olympic Committee founded the World Anti-Doping Agency (WADA) as an independent foundation. What an athlete can take before and during competition is now heavily regulated. Some drugs to treat a cold are permitted during training but not competition. Athletes that require drugs like insulin and testosterone for medical conditions are still permitted to take them, provided that they and their medical team have completed a Therapeutic Usage Exemption Certificate.

Private Collection

Blood capsules

During a rugby match in 2009, Harlequins winger Tom Williams bit into a fake blood capsule. His plan was to allow a specialist kicker onto the pitch as his 'blood replacement'. To help ensure that onlookers were convinced that his injury was genuine, when being attended to on the pitch he asked the team doctor to cut his lip. The substitution was subsequently made and his team gained an unfair advantage.

Private Collection

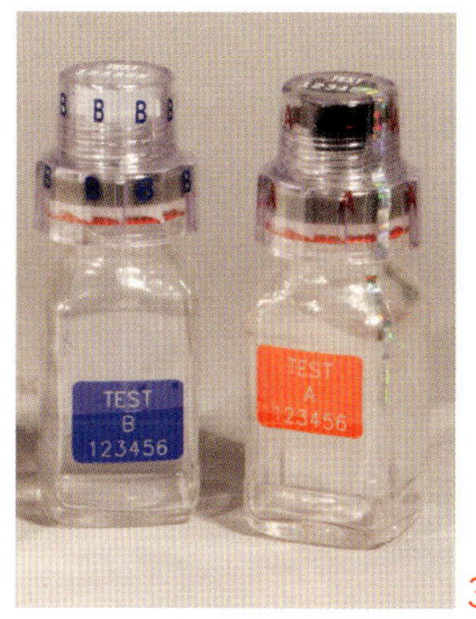

34

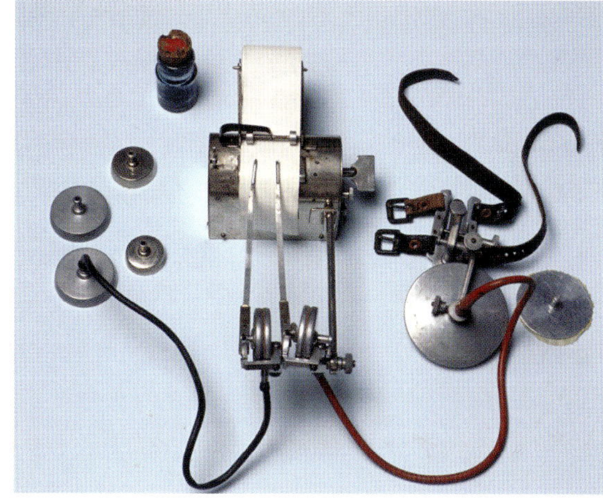

35

Specimen jars used in the drug testing of athletes [34]

UK Anti-Doping Monitors check on drug use in sport in Scotland. Elite athletes are part of the National Register Testing Pool (NRTP) and are obliged to provide a location (3 months in advance) detailing a 1-hour slot for every day of the year when they will be available for testing.

Private Collection

Polygraph machine [35]

Sir James MacKenzie (1853–1925) from Scone invented a way of recording pulses simultaneously from different parts of the body, and from the veins as well as arteries. He called his instrument a 'polygraph' because it had more than one receiver: one for the wrist and another moveable receiver which could be used on different parts of the body. The MacKenzie polygraph was an early forerunner of the lie detector, used today as a standard method to detect cheating in bodybuilding.

University of Dundee Museum Services, Tayside Medical History Museum

COMMISSIONING CONTEMPORARY ARTS FOR *HUMAN RACE*

Newly commissioned art works are an integral part of the Human Race exhibition. Contemporary arts can offer fresh, vivid and occasionally troubling perspectives on all parts of our world – including the rich material presented in this exhibition. The Human Race commissions will enhance the visitor's appreciation of the exhibition's themes as well as of wider issues surrounding the culture of sport.

The curators explored a range of art forms. The four selected artists – Louise Blamire, Beverley Hood, Kona McPhee and Catherine Street – use elements of performance, poetry, visual arts and new media. They entered the world of sport science and medicine in Scotland, all for the first time, in order to learn and be inspired by its current activity and its historical collections.

Rather than illustrating Scottish sport science and medicine, the artists were free to find inspiration in specific objects from existing Scottish sport science and medicine collections – and we are very grateful for the support and access they were given. They could find their own stories and angles, and express them as they wished. They were fascinated by the strong personalities, both living and dead, and the vivid stories, true and mythical, that they discovered. The works also point to the many tensions that exist in sport, within technology, science and training regimens. The founder of the modern Olympic movement, Pierre de Coubertin, spoke of the athlete as 'a moving sculpture' in an age of aspiration and hope, but perhaps we need more complex images for today.

The work you see here offers alternatives to the conventions of sport science and medicine, and shows this highly visible subject through a wider emotional lens. We hope this will encourage audiences to explore what really matters to them in that space between sport and medicine. The selected artists have created a new and striking set of artefacts that will outlast the Scottish touring exhibition and act as this creative partnership's legacy for years to come.

Professor Andrew Patrizio

COMMISSIONED ARTISTS

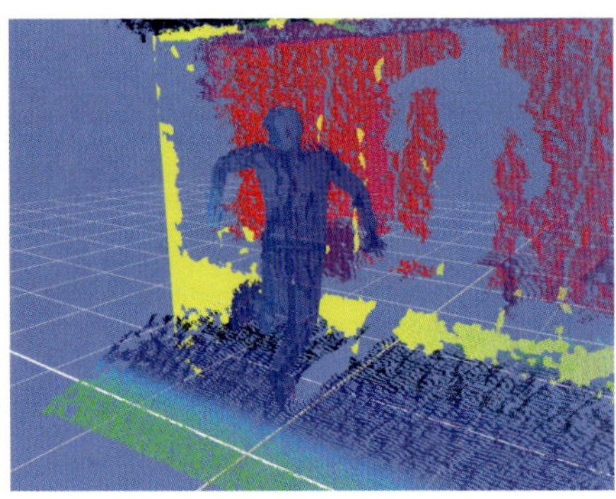

'glitching'

Beverley Hood has spent the past fifteen years creating digital arts projects that interrogate the impact of the virtual on the body, relationships and human experience. She studied sculpture and electronic imaging at Duncan of Jordanstone College of Art, Dundee and Nova Scotia College of Art & Design, Canada. Beverley is currently Postgraduate Lecturer in the School of Design at Edinburgh College of Art.

'glitching' is an ambitious digital installation and performance project commissioned for the Human Race exhibition. It attempts to re-describe the movement derived from characters in contemporary sports and action computer games.

As the gaming world grows ever more sophisticated and ubiquitous, the movements of characters become more and more 'realistic' and convincing, thanks to constant improvements in software and hardware. Often derived from the real (using motion capture and body scanning of professional sports players, for example), gaming characters of the 21st century have an extraordinary embodiment, fluidity of movement and naturalness. However, there are always imperfections and glitches, and it is these that interest

Credits:

Artist
Beverley Hood

Choreographer/Dancer
Tony Mills

Dancers
Hannah Seignior
and Felicity Beveridge

Installation soundtrack
Video Computer System
by Golden Shower

Composer
(performance soundtrack)
Martin Parker

Kinect and Unity Programming
Hemal Bodasing

Motion Capture and 3D Assistance
Chris Davies

Beverley. Whether through unexpected programming errors or the users' inability to control the characters in seamless game-play (resulting in bumping into walls, misfiring, etc) there is still the potential for awkwardness between spells of perfection.

Beverley has focused on the artificial nature of these glitches by employing highly trained real bodies to re-stage them – bodies such as that of Tony Mills, a professional break-dancer with an extraordinary ability to interpret and create fluid, awkward and extreme movements. Beverley is interested in how real bodies cope with, and interpret via sequences of choreography, the limits of such foreign and unnatural movement. By taking the digital and transplanting it, re-interpreting it, embodying it within the physical body – literally re-enacting it – does it disintegrate, transform, and become something new? Does it add something to our vocabulary of movement/ physicality/ humanity? In 'glitching' Beverley explores how this physically re-enacted choreography can be embedded and re-imaged within a 'live' digital environment, for an audience to interact with. Using the premise of home entertainment dance and training games (such as Just Dance, Zumba Fitness and Your Shape: Fitness Evolved), she has employed the motion-sensor controller, Microsoft Kinect, and large-screen display to create a digital installation with which the public can interact. The exhibition visitor is invited to step into the digital shoes of the 'lead dancer', and attempt to follow the awkward and intricate, glitch choreography performed by the dancing troupe on screen.

Alongside the Human Race exhibition there will be a series of 'glitching' live performances featuring the digital installation, dancers Tony Mills, Hannah Seignior, Felicity Beveridge, and a performance soundtrack devised by Martin Parker. These events will be advertised throughout the exhibition's wider events programme.

'glitching' was created as an Artist's Commission awarded by the Scotland & Medicine partnership. Additional funding was provided by a **Visual Artist's Award from Creative Scotland** and a **Research Award from Edinburgh College of Art**.

COMMISSIONED ARTISTS

Catherine Street

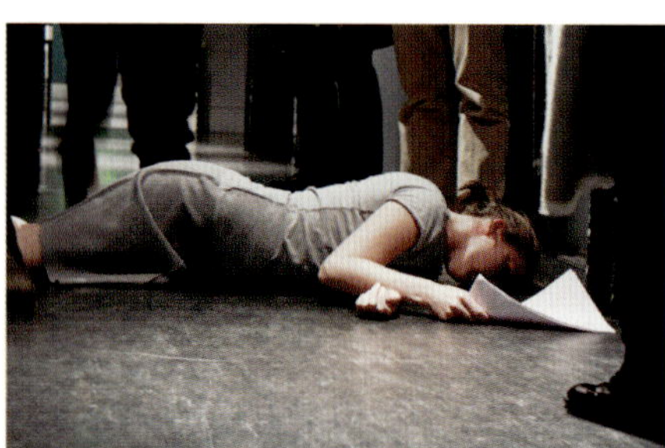

Catherine Street, performance commissioned by *cabin:codex*, Centre for Artists' Books at DJCAD. Photo: Ross Fraser McLean

Catherine Street's installations are pervasive and dramatic. Layering elements of video, sound, drawing, collage, text and performance, she creates potent and atmospheric environments. Street's own body is often present on film and in actuality, undertaking tasks of endurance and repetition. A viewer entering such environments, and encountering this body, is liable to feel a strong emotional response of some sort – unease, repulsion, fascination, surprise, exhilaration, even hilarity.

Continuing her interest in the complex relationship between mind and body, for this new work Street began by exploring the area of sport psychology. The concept of 'flow', a mental state which, although experienced rarely, is thought by some to be the optimum state for athletic performance, is a thread that runs through the work. This elusive state of mind is sometimes described in almost mystical terms, and apparently emerges from activities that may be repetitive or involve extreme endurance or concentration.

Whilst the physical and psychological limits of many people are only ever tested in situations that are not of their choosing, sport is one of the few public arenas where voluntary exposure to pain is accepted; at the same time, punishing training regimens often involve mundane, repetitive routines. Street is interested in the way in which people test their physical and psychological limits, and the situations in which we may witness them doing so. In much of her work she is also thinking about the limits of representing or speaking about the experiences of others, or even of ourselves.

About the video: Stress position/Ski sit

The 'wall sit' or 'ski sit' is a strengthening exercise for the quadriceps. The legs are bent to 90 degrees and the back is kept flat against the wall. The lower legs should be perpendicular to the floor. Street is thinking about the awkward role of the artist who carries out a physical or psychological task for the purpose of making his or her work.

About the drawings

The drawings were made in groups of four, with each individual drawing taking three hours to complete and the whole set of four executed in a twelve-hour period. They are a record of the repetitive making of tiny marks over a specified period of time. The drawings are shown alongside sound recordings that include a description of the experience of flow.

For more information about the artist, see catherinestreetartist.wordpress.com

COMMISSIONED ARTISTS

survival's dog-eat-dog
made literal, the trimmings
went to Mertz and Mawson
– forcing down those
pounds of husky liver,
sliver by revolting sliver

Extract from *'Meat'* by Kona Macphee

Kona Macphee

Kona Macphee grew up in Australia, where she experimented with a range of occupations, including composer, violinist, waitress and motorcycle mechanic. Eventually she took up robotics and computer science, which brought her to Cambridge as a graduate student in 1995. She now lives in Crieff, Perthshire, where she works as a freelance writer and moonlights as the co-director of a software and consultancy company.

As her erratic career path might suggest, Kona has always been equally interested in the humanities and the sciences. In an age of relentless specialisation, there aren't many niches left for generalists – but happily, writing poetry can be one of them. A poem can take its inspiration from anything, and borrow its imagery from anywhere: not only the inner emotional landscape of the poet, but the physical universe outside, the whole cacophonous spectrum of human thought and the wildest flourishes of the imagination. For Kona, getting to work means walking to her shed at the bottom of the garden – but, as she says, 'who knows where I might end up after that?'

When Kona was a child, she spent many happy hours poring over forensic pathology textbooks and related tomes like the quirky late-19th century compendium *Anomalies and Curiosities of Medicine* (perhaps this explains The Book of Diseases, a poem sequence inspired by human diseases that featured in her second collection *Perfect Blue*). Given this childhood fascination with matters biomedical, it was a particular pleasure for Kona to be commissioned by Human Race to produce a series of poems – not least because she got a personal tour of the closed collection at the Surgeons' Hall Museum in Edinburgh, which she says 'enthralled my inner (morbidly curious) ten-year-old.'

Kona believes that the most interesting ideas and inventions tend to emerge at the intersection of different disciplines. An example is the exciting field of biomimetics, where design and engineering take their inspiration from technologies that have evolved in nature, such as the way that individual strands on a bird's feather zip together. She says, 'I find there's a related fruitfulness in poetry commissions, where the craft and thematic preoccupations of the poet meet the particular context of the commission. I'm constantly surprised and delighted by the way that the external source material and the poetic sensibility can come together, often from very different starting points, to produce poems that are themselves full of unexpected and satisfying connections.'

Kona was particularly happy to find a home in the poem Meat, for the story of Australian explorer Douglas Mawson and his fateful Antarctic expedition. 'The fact that the poem was actually inspired by a footballer with a steak in his boot perfectly epitomises the unexpected directions in which a commission can take you as a writer.'

Kona has two poetry collections published by Bloodaxe Books, *Tails* (2004) and *Perfect Blue* (2010), which won the Geoffrey Faber Memorial Prize for 2010. More information is available at konamacphee.com.

COMMISSIONED ARTISTS

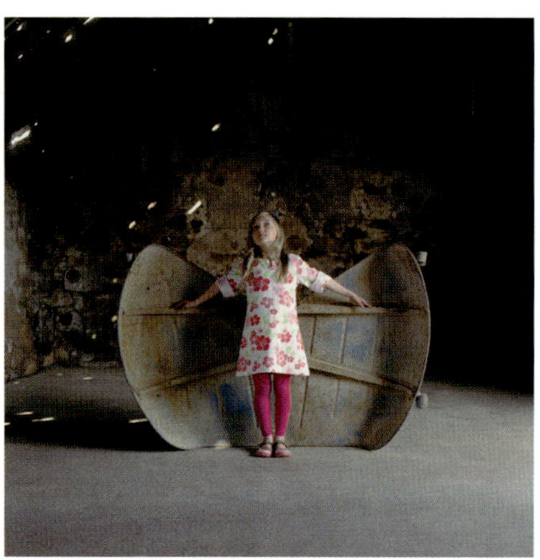

Louise Blamire

Louise grew up in the Scottish Borders and had an interesting and varied career before becoming a photographer and artist. Amongst other things, she has been a groom, a qualified nurse, a customer services manager and an international sports player, as well as being a mother.

Throughout her life and career, she says, 'art, in different forms, had beckoned but I didn't quite get to grips with it. I didn't know what I wanted to do or how I wanted to do it. I loved the feel of drawing implements. I loved splashing paint around paper and canvas. I loved writing diaries. But all these had limitations, or I had limitations. There never seemed to be a way of recording or articulating the things I felt I wanted or needed to. Then life's dictation chose my tool: the camera. It is like a black box flight recorder of life, which gave me the power to decide what I wanted people to see from the journey that I, its carrier, took.'

Louise graduated from Edinburgh College of Art in 2011 with a First Class Honours degree in photography and is still discovering how she will express her art through the lens. Or as she says, 'knowing what I want from it is still an on-going and organic process. No doubt, in time, it will show me.'

Louise begins most of her work in familiar environments, usually in and around her home. She uses metaphors and staged photography, from still life to small *tableaux* vivants. Natural light plays an important part in all of her work: she constructs the image around the natural light source and the space it penetrates. Another key characteristic of her work is the way in which she often incorporates people into an image with objects of interest she has gathered, or objects she has found in the immediate vicinity.

Louise was attracted to the Human Race project as soon as she visited the website. She says: 'I couldn't fail to be excited about the prospect of being involved. Human Race will enable me to bring together my nursing and sporting background in my photography. I feel like I have been given the opportunity to talk about and explore all the things I knew were important to me while growing up and starting out in my nursing career. As an athlete I understood the importance of performing and healing well: the need for professional medical care, good equipment, and the research involved to further the ability of the athlete, physically and psychologically. I am now in the fortunate position of being able to access the knowledge within sport science and medicine from a completely different vantage point.'
For more information about
Louise see louiseblamire.co.uk

SCOTTISH MEDICAL COLLECTIONS

The British Medical Ultrasound Society

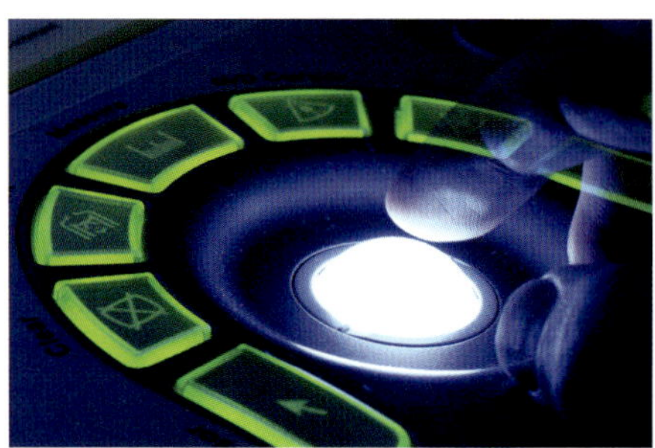

The British Medical Ultrasound Society (BMUS) is the leading UK body supporting the training and professional development of medical ultrasound practitioners, researchers and sonographers in the UK. The Society originated in 1969 from a conference organised by the Hospital Physicists Association (a predecessor of the Institute of Physics & Engineering in Medicine) and the British Institute of Radiology. The Society began as an informal group called the British Medical Ultrasound Group. In 1977 it was affiliated to the European and World Federations of Societies for Ultrasound in Medicine and became the British Medical Ultrasound Society.

Historical collection

The BMUS historical collection is held in Glasgow and provides a fascinating insight into the development of medical ultrasound. It was established in 1984 to collect, document, preserve, exhibit and interpret artefacts and other material relating to diagnostic and therapeutic ultrasound in the UK. The considerable collection includes ultrasound-related hardware such as small scanners and transducers as well as photographs, films and video. The collection also has a large manuscript archive containing, amongst other

Contact details:

BMU Historical Collection
Ultrasound Department
Derriford Hospital
Plymouth PL6 8DH
Tel: 01752 7633256
Web: www.bmus.org

BMUS General Secretary
The British Medical
Ultrasound Society (BMUS)
36 Portland Place
London W1B 1LS
Tel: 020 7636 3714
Email: secretariat@bmus.org
or office@bmus.org
Web: www.bmus.org

things, personal accounts, letters, original papers, interviews and books.

The historical documents and manuscripts are housed in the Mitchell Library archives. Some hardware items are on display at the Queen Mother's Hospital and larger items are stored at the Hunterian Museum, University of Glasgow and other institutions throughout the city.

Contributing to the collection

The Society is keen to continue to build and develop this unique collection and material of all types relating to all aspects of medical ultrasound is welcome. If you have anything to contribute please contact Chris Haydon or the BMUS General Secretary (see contact details left). Of particular importance and interest are documents and papers not normally kept by libraries.

Ultrasound and the 2012 Olympics

Ultrasound in the body travels 123-times faster than Usain Bolt, providing the fastest way to diagnose sporting injuries in athletes at the 2012 Olympics. Behind the scenes, a hidden team of musculoskeletal specialists and sonographers will be equipped with hi-tech portable ultrasound machines ready to image athletes' knees, wrists and ankles. Ultrasound provides higher resolution images of the joints than MRI and is ideally suited to detection of swelling, bruising and tears in muscles and tendons such as the Achilles tendon and rotator cuff. In the hands of appropriately trained sonographers, an ultrasound scanner becomes a valuable tool for the prevention, diagnosis and rehabilitation of sports injuries. Musculoskeletal ultrasound also plays a unique role in determining the mechanisms of sports injuries – not only locating the cause of an athlete's symptoms but identifying potential biomechanical faults, even before an injury has occurred. The portable nature of ultrasound also has the advantage of making repeated scanning of athletes possible in the stadium, or 'on site', to rapidly detect injuries or monitor their healing.

Access to the collections

The collections are housed in a number of institutions in Glasgow and are available to BMUS members and others for education, research and interest. If you wish to view or use the collection for exhibition or research, please contact Chris Haydon, Historical Collection Co-ordinator, or the BMUS General Secretary.

SCOTTISH MEDICAL COLLECTIONS

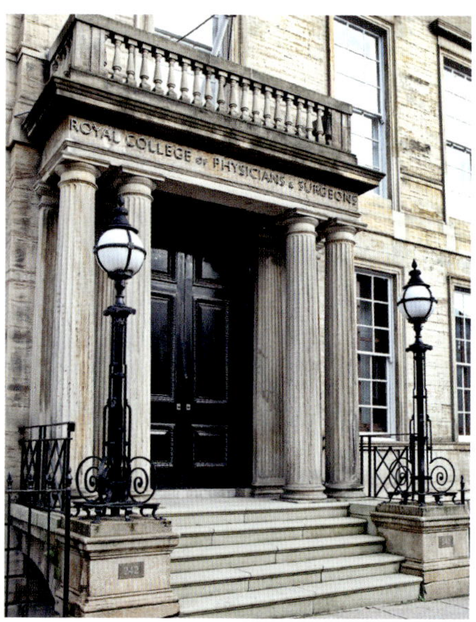

Royal College of Physicians and Surgeons of Glasgow

Founded in 1599, the RCPSG has a history spanning four centuries. The College enjoys a unique position amongst its sister Colleges in the UK in that its membership includes physicians, surgeons, dentists and specialists in the field of travel medicine.

The College's founder, Maister Peter Lowe, was a Scottish surgeon who had practised for a number of years in France. On his return to Scotland he was so horrified at the state of medical practice in Glasgow that he petitioned King James VI to be allowed to establish a regulatory body which would ensure that people acting as doctors (physicians and surgeons) in the city were properly trained. Today, the College offers career support to its membership through education, training, professional development, examinations and assessment, whilst acting as a charity and leading voice on health issues in order to set the highest standards of health care. Membership consists of over 10,000 practitioners worldwide.

In its long history the College has had several homes, initially meeting in different places such as Blackfriars' Kirk and Hutcheson's Hospital. The first Faculty Hall was established in

Contact details:
Carol Parry
Library and Heritage Manager
RCPSG
232–242 St Vincent Street
Glasgow G2 5RJ
Tel: 0141 2273234
Email: carol.parry@rcpsg.ac.uk
Web: www.rcpsg.ac.uk

the Trongate in 1698, followed by a move in 1791 to larger premises in St Enoch's Square. A further move was made in 1862 to the College's present building in St Vincent Street.

Library

With over 30,000 volumes, the library dates back to the building of the first Faculty Hall in 1698. The library committee was founded in 1768 and is the oldest committee in the College. With its earliest volume dating from 1491, the library now houses works on all aspects of medicine and surgery, including very fine and early examples of medical texts from the 16th and 17th centuries. Because of its close association with the city of Glasgow, the library has built up the Glasgow Collection, books relating to Glasgow and the West of Scotland.

Archives

The archives of the College date from the early 17th century. The first minute book starts in 1602 and the minutes run with just one gap (from 1688–1733 when a minute book was lost in a fire) up until the present day. The majority of the material dates from the 19th and 20th centuries, and includes examination registers, minutes and records relating to property, including plans of Faculty Hall designed by J.J. Burnet in 1892. A large photographic collection contains portraits of many 19th-century Fellows as well as covering more recent events. The archive is not a static entity and is being added to regularly so that the history of the College is preserved for future generations.

Instrument collection

Over the years, the College has acquired a collection of medical instruments dating from the 18th century right up to the present day. Items include the instruments of William Beatty (d.1842), surgeon aboard HMS Victory at the Battle of Trafalgar, a pocket set of instruments of the African explorer and missionary David Livingstone (1813–1873), and an operating table devised by the great Glasgow surgeon, Sir William Macewen (1848–1924).

Art collection

The art collection contains portraits of past presidents by famous Scottish artists such as Sir Henry Raeburn and Sir Daniel Macnee as well as an interesting and growing number of works by young and contemporary artists, many of which have been purchases from the annual exhibition of the Royal Glasgow Institute of Fine Arts.

SCOTTISH MEDICAL COLLECTIONS

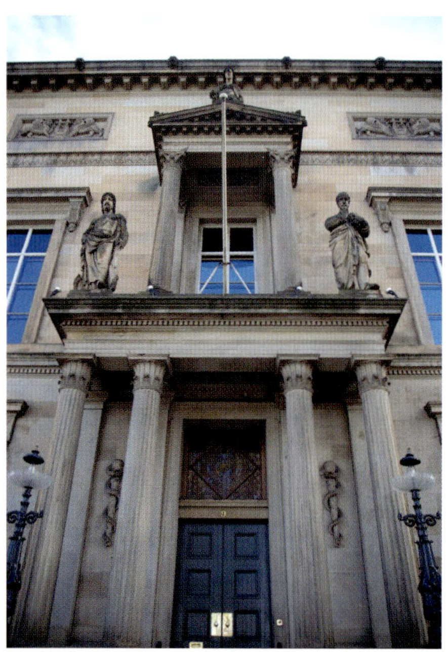

Royal College of Physicians of Edinburgh

The College

In the 17th century, Edinburgh physicians began to hold meetings in their own homes to discuss the regulation of medical practice and the ways in which standards in medicine could be improved. Sir Robert Sibbald, an eminent physician and noted historian, was a member of this group. He had the opportunity to petition King Charles II, who granted the Royal College of Physicians of Edinburgh its Royal Charter in 1681. Sir Robert is generally accepted to be the founder of the College.

The founding Fellows of the College were concerned not only with the advancement of medicine as a reputable science, but also with alleviating the miseries of the city's poor and needy.

For more than 300 years, the College has remained independent of control by government. The College's mission today lies close to the ideals of its founders: to promote the highest standards in internal medicine not only in Edinburgh where the College was founded and has developed, but wherever its Fellows and Members practise.

Contact details:
Royal College of
Physicians of Edinburgh
9 Queen Street
Edinburgh EH2 1JQ
Tel: 0131 225 7324
Fax: 0131 220 3939
Web: www.rcpe.ac.uk

The College acts in an advisory capacity to government and other organisations on many aspects of health and welfare and medical education. It was instrumental in founding the Royal Infirmary of Edinburgh and, over the years, has influenced the development of medical schools in North America, Australasia, Asia and Africa.

The Library

The Library of the Royal College of Physicians of Edinburgh was established in 1682 and was the first in Scotland specifically intended for the study of medicine. Sir Robert Sibbald, who had been the foremost figure in the creation of the College, donated 'three shelfes full of books to the Colledge of Physitians.' Since then the Library has provided over three-hundred years of continuous service to members of the College, and has grown into a comprehensive collection ranging from the earliest and rarest of medical writings to modern books, periodicals and online resources.

Access to the collections

The Library is open to the public. Please contact us to make an appointment.

SCOTTISH MEDICAL COLLECTIONS

The Royal College of Surgeons of Edinburgh

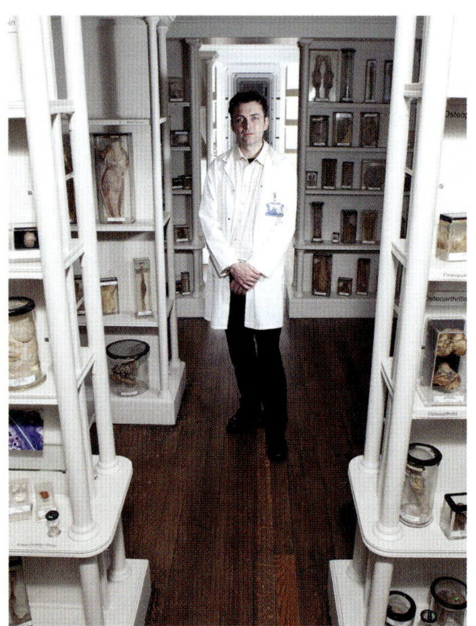

Contact details:
Surgeons' Hall Museum
The Royal College of Surgeons of Edinburgh
Nicolson Street
Edinburgh EH8 9DW
Tel: 0131 527 1649
Email: museum@rcsed.ac.uk
Web: www.museum.rcsed.ac.uk/

College Library and Archives
The Royal College of Surgeons of Edinburgh
Nicolson Street
Edinburgh EH8 9DW
Tel: 0131 527 1630 and 1632
Email: library@rcsed.ac.uk
Web: www.library.rcsed.ac.uk

Surgeons' Hall Museum

The Royal College of Surgeons of Edinburgh, founded in 1505, is the oldest medical institution of its kind in the world, and the College holds the largest collection of medical, anatomical and pathological material in Scotland, dating from Roman times to the present day.

Surgeons' Hall, designed by Sir William Playfair, opened in July 1832, the month before the first UK Anatomy Act became law. The entire upper floor of Surgeons' Hall was dedicated to the College's teaching collections of comparative anatomy and pathology. Although much of the comparative anatomy collection has been dispersed in the intervening years, the pathology collection has survived almost intact. It is probably one of the few early 19th-century medical museums in the world that still has most of its original collection on display and in the original space provided for it. It is Scotland's oldest medical museum.

Surgeons' Hall Museum includes early specimens from the College's first Anatomy and Pathology museum established in 1807; Sir Charles Bell's oil paintings of wounded soldiers from the Napoleonic Wars; David

Middleton Greig's skull collection; John Menzies Campbell's comprehensive dental collection; early microscopic preparations, microscopes and microtomes; historic anaesthetic and antisepsis equipment (including the most complete Squires II Inhaler known and a range of Lister carbolic spray machines); Lord Lister's frock coat and dissection kit; Sir James Young Simpson's top hat and medicine chest; original pathological drawings; X-rays, photographs and scans and over 3,000 surgical instruments dating back to classical times.

Displays show the methods for preservation and representation of the human body since 1505 and highlight developments and links between 'classical' surgery and contemporary specialisms such as reconstructive facial surgery and sports and exercise medicine. Displays on the notorious murderers Burke and Hare and the anatomist Dr Robert Knox include a wallet reputedly made out of the skin of William Burke. Multimedia access provides more in depth medical/surgical information and interdisciplinary cross-referencing.

Museum opening times:

Open to the public
Monday – Friday 12.00–4pm
Weekend opening April–October

Library and Archive

RCSEd library is one of the oldest medical libraries in Scotland. Collections include: historic and rare books including early anatomical atlases, medical and surgical texts dating from the 16th century and current medical/surgical journals, books and digital resources.

The archive holds the institutional records of the College dating from the early 16th century and private papers relating to famous medical pioneers including: Sir James Young Simpson, Joseph Bell (the inspiration for Sherlock Holmes), Joseph Lister and Sir Michael Woodruff.

Access to the collections

The Library is open to Members and Fellows 09.00–17.00 Monday–Friday General researchers by appointment.

SCOTTISH MEDICAL COLLECTIONS

University of Aberdeen

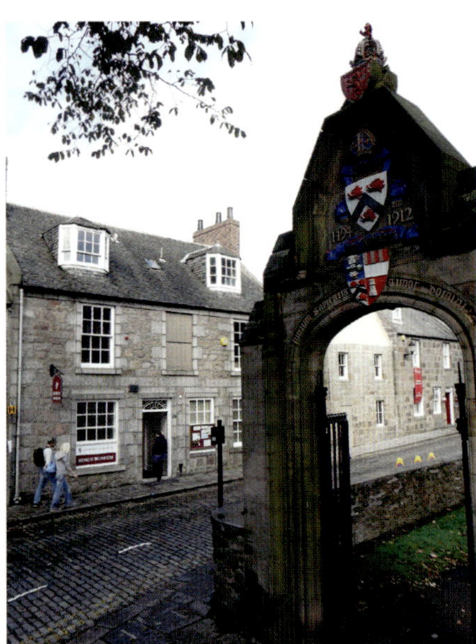

Anatomy Museum

The origins of the Anatomy Museum in Aberdeen are unclear but there is documentation which describes the opening of the refurbished Anatomy Museum at Marischal College in 1881 as part of a general refurbishment of the Anatomy department, at that time under the guidance of the first Regius Chair of Anatomy Professor John Struthers. Struthers was ahead of his time in terms of the needs of medical education and, following his retirement from Aberdeen, he went on to become the first Chair of the Medical Education Committee of the General Medical Council. Struthers was succeeded by Professor Robert W Reid, who occupied the Regius Chair of Anatomy from 1889–1925. Professor Reid was a skilled dissector and made a sizeable contribution to the cadaveric objects within the Anatomy Museum.

The collections are wide-ranging and the earliest specimens can be traced back to the 1870s. Collecting of objects for the museum has been driven by the research and teaching activities of staff over the years and the museum has some notable strengths: skeletal material, fluid-preserved specimens of human tissues, modern plastic anatomical models'

Contact details:

Anatomy Museum
University of Aberdeen
Suttie Centre
Foresterhill
Aberdeen AB25 2ZD
Tel: 01224 274320
Email: museums@abdn.ac.uk
Web: www.abdn.ac.uk/museums

King's Museum
University of Aberdeen
17 High Street
Old Aberdeen AB24 3EE
Email: kingsmuseum@abdn.ac.uk
Web: www.abdn.ac.uk//kingsmuseum

historical anatomical models (of wax, papier-mâché and plaster), and works on paper, including 19th-century watercolours and anatomical drawings by Alberto Morrocco. In addition, the museum has a small collection of associated material, like anti-grave-robbing devices used in the north-east of Scotland in the nineteenth century.

Access to the collections

Access to the collections is restricted.

King's Museum

Scotland's oldest – and newest – museum, the University of Aberdeen's King's Museum, is open throughout the year. On show are changing displays drawn from the university's collections, which are among the largest and most important in Scotland, having been awarded the status of a Recognised Collection on National Significance. Records of a museum in King's College date back to 1727. King's Museum houses exhibitions and activities which use the collections of Scottish archaeology and folk life, ethnography, Egyptian antiquities, numismatics and militaria, as well as from the University's science collections.

SCOTTISH MEDICAL COLLECTIONS

cont. **University of Aberdeen**

Special Collections

The University of Aberdeen was founded in 1495 and, until the 1970s, was the main repository for archival collections in the northern half of Scotland. A Special Collections department was formed in the 1960s to care for the University's unique and internationally significant range of printed, archival and other documentary sources. The richness of these collections extends across all the disciplines of the medieval and early modern university *curriculum* and across the European world of learning. Printed material comprises over 150,000 printed volumes, dating from the 1460s to the late 20th century, administered as four distinct chronological collections, which represent the evolution of the printed book and the University's unique legacy of over 500 years of learning; and 40 named collections, covering a wide variety of subjects, most of which have come to the University since the mid-19th century. Archival holdings include medical archives reflecting the University's expertise, from the late 19th century, in the allied fields of anatomy, physiology, pharmacology and pathology.

Contact details:
Special Collections Centre
University Library
Bedford Road
Aberdeen AB24 3AA
Tel: 01224 27 2598
Email: speclib@abdn.ac.uk
http://www.abdn.ac.uk/library/about/special/

King's Museum
University of Aberdeen
17 High Street
Old Aberdeen AB24 3EE
Tel: 01224 274330
Email: museums@abdn.ac.uk
Web: www.abdn.ac.uk/zoologymuseum

Zoology Museum

The Zoology Museum has the only large, internationally important collection of zoological specimens in the north of Scotland. The earliest reference to the collections dates from 1782. In his book, *A General Description of the East Coast of Scotland from Edinburgh to Cullen*, Francis Douglas wrote, 'Commencing about 1772 Professor William Ogilvie began of his own accord to put together a collection of specimens for a museum of natural history in the King's College, and has now fitted up, and furnished three apartments for their accommodation...' The collection was later at Marischal College and has been at its present location in Old Aberdeen since 1973.

The Zoology Museum cares for an extensive range of material, worldwide in scope, which covers the whole of the animal kingdom, from protozoa to the great whales. The collection contains around 75,000 specimens and it has resulted from over 200 years of collecting. Not only does it reflect the teaching and research interests of staff and students, but also the gifts of graduates and friends of the University.

Access to collections

Access information can be found on the website or by contacting the museum.

SCOTTISH MEDICAL COLLECTIONS

University of Dundee

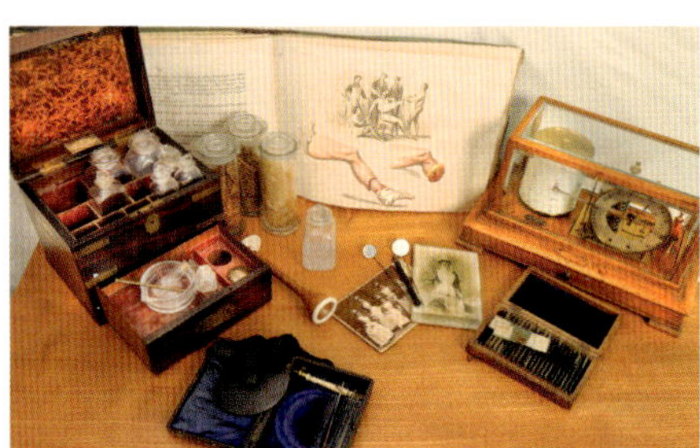

University of Dundee Archive Services

The University of Dundee Archives hold a wide variety of collections that contain a wealth of material for all types of researcher: academic staff, postgraduate and undergraduate students, private researchers, including family historians, and school pupils. The diversity of medicine-related research themes to be found within the collections is immense, and includes the history of insanity, tropical medicine, medical missions, surgery, pathology, infectious diseases and the experiences of women in the medical and nursing professions. These include documents and photographs from the Tayside Health Board in the Tayside area (asylums, hospitals, Boards of Management, Colleges of Nursing, for example); Dundee Dental Hospital; Manuscript Collections; and the University Records Collection, which contains the records of various medical professors and lecturers.

The collection houses various pathological materials, including drawings, engravings and photographs. The majority of the pathological drawings are by Neil Stewart and feature comments by Sir William Tennant Gairdner, the eminent pathologist and physician.

Contact details:

Archive, Records Management
University of Dundee
Dundee DD1 4HN
Tel: 01382 384095
Email: archives@dundee.ac.uk

University of Dundee Museum Services
Hawkhill House
University of Dundee
Dundee DD1 4HN
Tel: 01382 384310
Email: museum@dundee.ac.uk
Web: www.dundee.ac.uk/museum

Tayside Medical History Museum
c/o University of Dundee Museum Services
Hawkhill House, University of Dundee
Dundee DD1 4HN
Tel: 01382 384310
Email: museum@dundee.ac.uk
Web: www.dundee.ac.uk/museum/medical.htm

University of Dundee Museum Services

The University has a wide variety of museum collections acquired during the 130 years of the institution's existence, all of which are cared for by Museum Services, which stages regular exhibitions in the Tower Foyer and Lamb Galleries. These include scientific instruments, natural history, fine art and design. Collections of medical interest include models and instruments from the departments of Anatomy and Physiology, instruments and comparative anatomy specimens from the Dental School, instruments and equipment from Biological Sciences, and the D'Arcy Thompson Zoology Museum, named in honour of its founder, Professor D'Arcy Thompson, who was one of the principal founders of Dundee's Medical School. Museum Services is also jointly responsible for running the Tayside Medical History Museum.

Tayside Medical History Museum

Founded in 1989, the Tayside Medical History Museum is jointly managed by the University of Dundee Museum Services and NHS Tayside. Its collections represent the history of medicine and medical teaching in Dundee and Tayside over the past 200 years, and are displayed in both permanent displays and temporary exhibitions in the Medical School, Ninewells Hospital, as well as satellite displays in other hospitals around the region. The collections include surgical instruments, nursing medals and certificates, hospital equipment, plant medicines, early X-ray tubes and portraits of local medical personalities.

SCOTTISH MEDICAL COLLECTIONS

University of Edinburgh

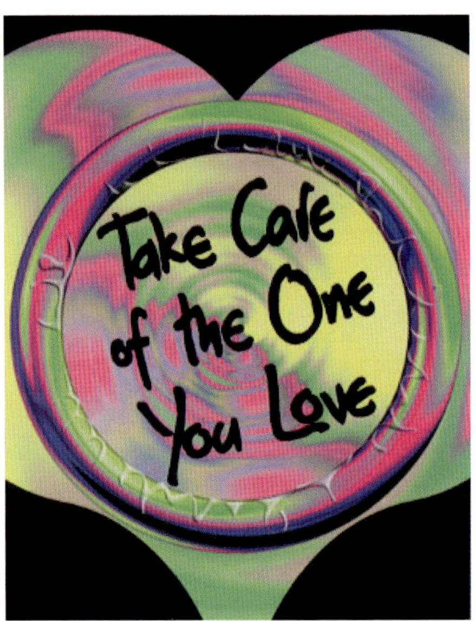

Courtesy of Lothian Health Services Archive, Edinburgh University Library

The University of Edinburgh has rich collections dating back from the seventeenth century. The collections include manuscripts, specimens, and iconic items such as William Burke's skeleton.

Special Collections

Special Collections includes Western medieval manuscripts, Oriental manuscripts, some 400,000 early and special printed books, architectural plans, photographs and drawings. There are extensive holdings of personal, business and literary papers, including many relating to Scottish medicine and science. In total we have over 30km of collections material.

Access to the collections

The collections are available to anyone. They are housed in the Centre for Research Collections on the 6th floor of Edinburgh University Main Library.

Contact details:
Centre for Research Collections,
Edinburgh University Library,
George Square,
Edinburgh EH8 9LJ
Tel: 0131 650 8379
Email: is-crc@ed.ac.uk
Web: www.ed.ac.uk/is/crc

Lothian Health Services Archive

Lothian Health Services Archive (LHSA) holds the historically important local records of NHS hospitals and other health-related material. LHSA collects, preserves and catalogues these records and promotes them to increase understanding of the history of health and for the benefit of all. LHSA is core-funded by NHS Lothian and project funded by a variety of institutions, including the Wellcome Trust. LHSA is part of the University of Edinburgh's Centre for Research Collections.

A variety of NHS clinical and non-clinical records are held dating from 1770 and 1594, respectively. Gifted or deposited non-NHS institutional and personal papers have increased the range and depth of holdings, which now occupy c.3,000 shelf metres. This rich collection also includes c.1 million folder-based clinical case notes and c.40,000 images, along with older printed books, pamphlets, objects, artwork and a small quantity of digital assets.

The significance of LHSA's Edinburgh and Lothian HIV/AIDS Collections has been recognised by a 2011 inscription to the UNESCO UK Memory of the World Register (www.lhsa.lib.ed.ac.uk/source/HIVAIDS_index.htm).

Access to the collections

Collections can be accessed by researchers and members of the public but are subject to legal restrictions. Details about access can be found at http://www.lhsa.lib.ed.ac.uk/services/index.html Images can be viewed on Flickr at www.flickr.com/photos/49439570@N08

Contact details:
Lothian Health Services Archive
Edinburgh University Main Library
30 George Square
Edinburgh, EH8 9LJ
Email: lhsa@ed.ac.uk
Tel: +44 (0)131 650 3392
Fax: +44 (0)131 650 2922
Web: www.lhsa.lib.ed.ac.uk
Blog: www.lhsa.blogspot.com
Facebook: www.facebook.com/lhsa.edinburgh

SCOTTISH MEDICAL COLLECTIONS

cont. **University of Edinburgh**

The Anatomical Museum

The Anatomical Museum, founded and developed by the Monro dynasty, flourished under Sir William Turner, Professor of Anatomy from 1867 to 1903, and Principal of the University from 1903 to 1917. Turner had broad interests in evolution and comparative anatomy, and built up the impressive collections displayed.

The splendid Museum Hall was at the heart of the new Medical School designed by the architect Robert Rowand Anderson. It opened with great ceremony in 1884.

In the 1950s, the three-storey Museum Hall was reduced to a single upper storey, which still survives as the museum.

Access to the collections

Opening hours vary, check the website for details. Admission is free.

Contact details:
Anatomical Museum
University of Edinburgh
Doorway 3
Medical School
Teviot Place
Edinburgh
EH8 9XD
Web: www.anatomy.mvm.ed.ac uk/museum/index.php

SCOTTISH MEDICAL COLLECTIONS

University of Glasgow

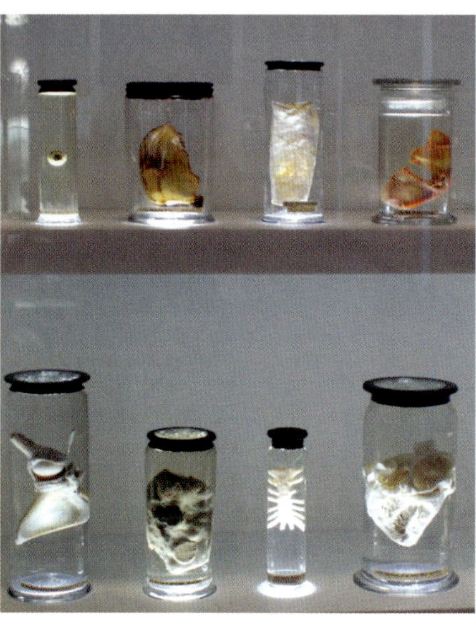

The Hunterian

The Hunterian was opened to the public in 1807 and is Scotland's oldest public museum. It was established around the collections of Dr William Hunter, the celebrated 18th-century anatomist, doctor and obstetrician. As a physician and collector, he was unique amongst his contemporaries in several ways, not least in having had the foresight to bequeath his entire museum collections and library to his *alma mater*, the University of Glasgow, thereby avoiding their dispersal in the salerooms. Hunter also bequeathed £8,000 for the construction of a suitable museum.

Hunter's collections were wide-ranging, containing coins, paintings, minerals, shells, anatomical and natural history specimens, printed books and manuscripts. The core of the collections is the anatomical preparations made by Hunter and his pupils. This material differs from all other parts of his collection in that it was made and used by Hunter for teaching and research work throughout his long, successful medical career. The anatomical material comprises wet preparations of human, and some animal, tissues and organs, skeletal material, air-dried preparations and some animal taxidermy specimens.

Contact details:

Maggie Reilly, The Hunterian
University of Glasgow
Glasgow G12 8QQ
Tel: 0141 330 4221
Email: Maggie.Reilly@.glasgow.ac.uk
Web: www.hunterian.gla.ac.uk

Prof AP Payne, Laboratory of Human Anatomy
Thomson Building
University of Glasgow G12 8QQ
Tel: 0141 330 5871
Email: A.Payne@bio.gla.ac.uk
Web: www.gla.ac.uk/schools/lifesciences/aboutus/themuseumofanatomy

The medical collections have a long and complex history reflecting the intricacies of the history of the University. They were considerably supplemented throughout the 19th century and 20th centuries with new specimens being added by University teaching and research staff. The post-Hunter material includes comparative (animal) anatomy specimens, fine 19th-century wax models and specimens made using recent techniques such as corrosion and plastination. The Hunter anatomical collections were moved to the Department of Anatomy in 1901 and were further sub-divided in 1954 when the pathology (morbid anatomy) specimens were removed to the University Department of Pathology at the Glasgow Royal Infirmary in the centre of the city. However, in 2012, the pathology collections are to be reunited with the anatomy material.

The Hunterian collections also include medical equipment and instruments. Highlights here include Hunter's own instruments, Joseph Lister's equipment and the teaching collections of the former Glasgow College of Nursing.

Access to the collections

Parts of the medical collections are on show in the permanent exhibitions, 'Healing Passion' and 'William Hunter: Man, Medic and Collector' at the main Hunterian Museum, and also in the teaching Museum of Anatomy in the Thomson Building on the main campus at the University of Glasgow.

SCOTTISH MEDICAL COLLECTIONS

University of Glasgow

cont.

University of Glasgow Library, Special Collections

Glasgow University's Special Collections Department is one of the foremost resources in Scotland for academic research and teaching. Built up over a period of more than 500 years by purchase, gift and bequest, the collections now contain more than 200,000 manuscripts items and around 200,000 printed works, including over 1,000 incunabula.

Probably the best known of the Library's rare book collections, the Hunterian Library contains some 10,000 printed books and 650 manuscripts, and forms one of the finest 18th-century libraries to survive intact. It was assembled by Dr William Hunter. Under the terms of Hunter's will, his library and other collections remained in London for several years after his death – for the use of his nephew, Dr Matthew Baillie (1761–1823) – and finally came to the University in 1807.

About one-third of Hunter's books – not unnaturally – are to do with medicine, with a good balance struck between the great historical texts (such as editions of Hippocrates, Galen, Vesalius, Harvey) and the writings of his own contemporaries (men like

Contact details:
Special Collections
Glasgow University Library
Hillhead Street
Glasgow G12 8QE
Tel: 0141 330 6767
Email: special@lib.gla.ac.uk
Web: http://special.lib.gla.ac.uk/

Smellie, the Monros, Albinus, Haller). Anatomy and obstetrics – the two fields in which Hunter made his fame and fortune – are particularly well represented; though an interest in other topics such as naval medicine, the deficiency diseases and inoculation against smallpox, is also represented.

Access to the collections

Semester opening hours:
Monday to Thursday: 9.00–19.00
Friday: 10.00–17.00
Vacation opening hours:
Monday to Thursday: 9.00–17.00
Friday: 10.00–17.00

SCOTTISH MEDICAL COLLECTIONS

University of St Andrews

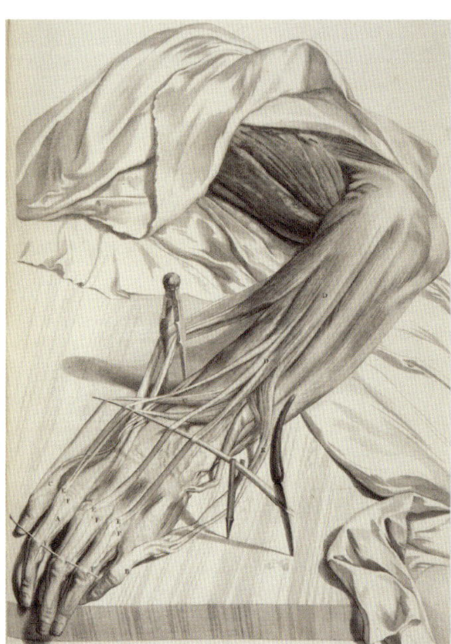

Govard Bidloo, *Anatomia Humani Corporis* (Amsterdam, 1685).

Anatomy and Pathology Collection

The Anatomy and Pathology Collection contains over 5,000 items, mainly gross wet and dry specimens, but also surgical instruments, wax and plastinated models, and teaching charts, some of the latter being produced by local artists. Particular highlights include the collection of 91 incredibly detailed wax and plaster models of specific parts of the body, produced by companies such as Tramond of Paris in the late 19th century. The Collection also contains material such as the nine original watercolour drawings of a progressive dissection of the trunk and inguinal regions, produced by David Waterston, Professor of Anatomy 1914–1942, and artist J.T. Murray, and published as plates in the standard anatomical textbook, *Anatomy in the Living Model*, London, 1931. The Collection, including the historical models, is used for teaching in the University's School of Medicine. It illustrates the development of teaching and research in the field of anatomy at the University of St Andrews, and is of professional interest to anatomists generally.

Access to the collection

Admission is free but, due to the nature of the collections, access is subject to

Contact details:
Curator of the Anatomy
and Pathology Collection
Medical and Biological Sciences Building
University of St Andrews
North Haugh, St Andrews
Fife KY16 9TF
Tel: 01334 463551
Email: sw1s@st-andrews.ac.uk
Web: www.st-andrews.ac.uk/museum/

legal restrictions, and is by appointment only to legitimate enquirers.

Special Collections Department

The Department of Special Collections is home to the Library's collections of rare and early printed books, manuscripts, photographs and the University's institutional archive (muniments). These form a superb resource for research and teaching in a wide variety of disciplines across the arts and sciences. The rare book collections include anatomical atlases and medical texts from the 15th century onwards, as well as the personal libraries of two medical practitioners: Sir John Wedderburn (1599–1679), physician to Charles I, and James Simson (1740–1770), second Chandos Professor of Medicine at the University. The manuscript collection includes medical lecture notes, H G Callan's research on lampbrush chromosomes, reports of medical health officers in Fife, an army surgeon's journals from 19th-century India, hospital administrative records, accounts for medical treatments and recipes for home remedies.

Testimonials written in support of those applying to the University for the award of an MD degree form the most significant medical resource within the University's archives. Covering 1718–1894, these were usually provided to the Senatus by practising doctors in support of named individuals and can be anything from formulaic testimonials of worthiness to full personal histories. Doctors in receipt of the St Andrews MD by testimonial included Jean-Paul Marat (1775), Edward Jenner (1792), and Nelson's surgeon at Trafalgar, William Beatty (1817). Both testimonials and minutes of the Senatus are heavily used for family history and biographical research.

Access to collections

As reader space is very limited, access to the Reading Room is strictly by appointment only. Please contact us in advance to make an appointment.

Contact details:
Department of Special Collections
Library Annexe
North Haugh, St Andrews
Fife KY16 9WH
Tel: 01334 462339
Email: speccoll@st-andrews.ac.uk
Web: www.st-andrews.ac.uk/library/specialcollections/

ACKNOWLEDGEMENTS

Rami Abboud
Rohan Almond
Brian Bartlett
Emma Black
Louise Blamire
Michael Bolik
Neil Braidwood
Andrew Connell
Sylvie Coupland
Neil Curtis
Sarah Deans
Paul Dimeo
Jennifer Downes
Jeff Dunn
Shona Elliott
Thomas Elliott
David Fingland
John Fleming
Alastair Forbes
David Gaimster
Fiona Gilbert
Yvonne Gilbert
Ian Gow
Phillip Graham
Dee Halil
Anette Hagan
Graeme Hancock
Tracey Hawkins
Elizabeth Henderson
Chris Henry
Ruth Honeybone
Beverley Hood
Angela Howe
Peggy Hughes
Baljit Jagpa
Matthew Jarron
Craig Johnstone
Dawn Kemp
David Kerr
Steven Kerr
Steve Kilpatrick
Kirsten Lloyd
Jane Lumsden
Ellen McAdam
Richard McBrearty
Kona Macphee
Robyn Marsak
Iain Milne
Jullie Morow
Teresa Morris
Kevin Murray
Malcolm Nicholson
Joanne O'Hara
Carol Parry
Alan Pert
Alison Pert
Laurie Rae
Maggie Reilly
Ross Saunders
Francis W. Smith
Marianne Smith
Catherine Street
Elaine Stewart
Neil Symington
Alastair Tough
Anne Wade
Daniel Warren
Nicholas Watson

SCOTLAND & MEDICINE:
Collections & Connections Partners

City of Edinburgh Council
Edinburgh College of Art
Fife Council
High Life Highland
Hunterian Museum and Art Gallery, University of Glasgow
Lothian Health Services Archive
NHS Health Scotland
National Galleries of Scotland
National Library of Scotland
Royal College of Physicians of Edinburgh
Royal College of Physicians and Surgeons of Glasgow
Royal College of Surgeons of Edinburgh
Royal Scottish Academy
Scottish Borders Council
University of Aberdeen (Marischal Museum)
University of Dundee
University of Edinburgh
University of Dundee

VENUE PARTNERS:

Aberdeen Sports Village
City Art Centre, Edinburgh
Inverness Museum and Art Gallery
Institute of Sport and Exercise, University of Dundee
The Peak at Stirling Sports Village
Royal Commonwealth Pool, Edinburgh
University of Aberdeen
University of Dundee
University of Stirling

Our apologies to those we have missed, our gratitude is no less.